CW01574391

CAST OUT—BUT NOT FORSAKEN

RSGT

CAST OUT
—but not forsaken

Janice Wiseman

Bryntirion Press
1998

First published 1998
ISBN 1 85049 148 8

Cover design: Phil Boorman
Cover Illustration: D. J. Wiseman

Typeset by Tentmaker Publications, Stoke-on-Trent.

Published by Bryntirion Press,
Bryntirion, Bridgend, CF31 4DX, Wales, UK

Printed by WBC Book Manufacturers, Bridgend, Wales.

Foreword

BACK in the early 1980s, when I was a Methodist Minister in a little Yorkshire mill town, a newly-married couple began to attend my church. They were not exactly young, though the wife, a vivacious dark-eyed woman, seemed much younger than her husband. Both were smart, likeable, intelligent and deeply committed to the Lord Jesus Christ. At the same time I sensed that both had already led full lives before God brought them together. Just how full a life Janice Wiseman, the wife, had led, becomes apparent in these pages. Later, they joined a fellowship group which my wife and I ran at the manse, and it was after one of these meetings that we prayed for the baby boy that Janice was carrying, with results that I'll leave you to discover as you read the story!

It was not long before we moved away, and our paths have not often crossed since then, but Janice has kept in touch with us, and it has been a delight to discover how she has been carving out a ministry for herself as a Christian writer—and it is a ministry. The book you now have in your hand is a collection of scenes from her life-story, a wide-ranging pilgrimage as God led this feisty, somewhat rebellious girl out of her Jewish home, into a distinguished career as a Christian missionary in India, brutally cut short by illness, then through a wilderness period after her return home, followed by her meeting with her husband, a growing tranquillity, and then reconciliation with her parents.

Sometimes the story she tells is hilarious, sometimes

upsetting, but it is always interesting, and one thing is certain: when you pick up the book, give yourself plenty of time, because you really won't be able to put it down!

Rev. David Collinson
Superintendent Methodist Minister
Aberdeen, Scotland

Preface

AS I reflect upon my life how fitting are A.W. Tozer's words, 'If it is good God did it. And if it is bad I did it.'

As a modem Jewess, tenaciously setting out to follow the beckoning call of the Messiah, how could I have anticipated the twists and turns of the road ahead? A shocked and scandalised family, a three-month Euro-Asian trek in the bemused company of a half-dozen Australian adventurers, a medical and spiritual mission to India, a healing from diabetes, a son in 'old age'—all this and much more in 'CAST OUT—but not forsaken.'

May this book encourage you to pray that many more Jewish sons and daughters shall place their faith in our Lord Jesus, the Messiah, for the whole family of God is blessed more abundantly with the fulfilment of that ancient promise to Abraham, "All peoples on earth will be blessed through you" (Genesis 12:3). Hallelujah!

My thanks and appreciation to my beloved husband who has encouraged and helped me in the preparation of this book, and to our son for his long-suffering.

Praise and thanksgiving, above all, to God himself, Father, Son and Holy Spirit, who makes all things possible in his love.

To protect a few of those mentioned in the book, I have changed some of the names. Otherwise, it is as completely factual as my memory will allow.

To Matthew

Stand firm and hold to the teachings
we passed on to you.

2 Thessalonians 2:15

Table of Contents

CHAPTER ONE

'Buried Alive?'

MY marble headstone in the Jewish cemetery read:

JANICE REBECCA WISEMAN
MAY 1946 – FEBRUARY 1963

And yet I was still very much alive!

In 1964, exactly one year after my being baptised as a Christian, it suddenly occurred to me that my rabbinic grandfather may possibly have urged my parents, along with the backing of the strict Hebrew community, to erect a small marble headstone within the perimeter of the Jewish cemetery.

Too afraid to visit the cemetery myself, I approached Lois, a single gentile friend of mine in her middle twenties.

'Lois,' I asked, 'when you drop in to visit your parents would you do me a favour, please?'

She nodded. 'If I can.'

'Would you go along and look for a headstone in the Jewish cemetery?'

Her blue eyes opened wide. 'A what?' she gasped. 'A headstone. Who's headstone, for goodness sake?'

'Mine,' I replied, with a frown.

'Yours!' she exclaimed. 'Is this some kind of silly, sick joke?'

How hard it was to fully explain to an outsider the ultra-Orthodox Jewish ways and the harsh tradition of disowning one of 'Abraham's seed' who had chosen to become a follower of Jesus the Messiah.

I told Lois how the crunch came a year after my conversion, in 1963, when I was just seventeen, how I'd read in Acts 8:36-39 about the baptism of the Ethiopian eunuch and had decided I too would be baptised. Having approached Dr D. Martyn Lloyd-Jones, the then minister of London's Westminster Chapel, he suggested I should contact a Baptist minister in my home town of Wimbledon. The Doctor explained to me that, whilst he practised adult baptism, it was only by sprinkling. He knew I wanted to be fully immersed.

'Oh, my life! You mustn't do it, Jan,' begged my tearful Aunt Mag. 'You know full well that your parents will be absolutely heart-broken. And as for your poor granddad... well, the shock could possibly finish him off.'

Taking little notice of her pleadings, I waited for the right moment when mum and dad were together in the same room. I hesitatingly informed them of my future plans to be baptised as a Christian believer.

Mum put aside her sewing and, with her piercing dark eyes, glared at me. 'If you go ahead with such a ritual in the Christian Church, then you cannot be our daughter any more. Do you understand?' she stated firmly in a loud voice, for it was clear to her that what I intended to do was similar to a Jew being mikvahed—a form of ritual cleansing by immersion in the synagogue, initially declaring oneself to be a Jew.

I shook my head. 'That's horrid, really awful. Can't you even begin to see it from my point of view? I consider I shall be doing this as a form of witness,' I replied. 'For me, it would be disobedient not to be baptised.'

Her concern was how the immediate family were going to show their faces in the Jewish community. 'And what on earth will all our neighbours say?'

'Blow the wretched neighbours! What do you think this will do to my new grocery business?' dad remarked, looking worried. 'Who will want to come and buy from me, the father of a crazy Jesus worshipper?'

'You might do very well,' I interrupted, with a grin. 'Customers might turn up in droves for you might be seen as some sort of a novelty, a bit like the monkeys in the zoo!' My vain attempt at humour didn't exactly go down too well.

My grandfather, Sir John Flowers, who was an elderly Cantor rabbi, had been asleep in the next room. He awoke to hear the shouting and came to join in. 'You upset everyone!' he boomed, red in the face, furiously flaying his arms about. 'It is as if you've gone out of your way to make me, a rabbi, a laughing stock before the whole Hebrew congregation.'

My family shrank from the shame; understandably so, for it is always a disgraceful thing for a Jewish family to lose a member in this way. How I wished they'd have realised that my becoming a Messianic believer was not a denial of one's Jewishness, but a fulfilment of it.

On a chilly Sunday evening, dressed in reasonably warm clothing, I took my big bath towel and walked along to South Wimbledon Baptist Church.

During the baptismal service I sat in the front pew with a deacon's wife, Christine. As we sang the first hymn, 'Take my life and let it be,' I slowly turned my head. My eyes swept the congregation to see if any of my friends from Westminster Chapel were there, as promised, to support me and witness my baptism. Not one came. My eyes filling with tears, I gripped the end of the pew to steady myself, as if to keep hold of my faith somehow.

'No-one,' I murmured to Christine, my voice sounding strangely husky. 'I've got no-one', and again as though it were someone else who spoke. 'Me… I have no friends, and now I'll have no family.' Where was the joy I expected?

'Shh, don't let the devil get to you, Jan,' she whispered, interlacing her fingers with mine.

What does she know? I thought to myself. She's not Jewish.

The Baptist minister at the front of the church was making his way down the steps into the pool. As I blinked away the blinding tears, he came back into focus and beckoned to me.

I walked forward and down into the water; the minister gripped me, pushed me back, proclaiming, 'I baptise you in the name of the Father, Son and Holy Spirit.'

After the service the minister asked Gillian, one of the Baptist members, if she would give me a lift to my granddad's house in her car, for we were staying there whilst our own home was undergoing major repairs to the roof. She agreed as she lived only streets away from Parkside.

'Will you be all right?' Gillian asked, pulling up outside the large wrought iron gates through which one could see the house silhouetted against the dark evening sky.

I nodded.

I walked carefully along the gravel drive. A large dog barked loudly, startling me.

'Who's there?' shouted a man's gruff voice. It was Jake, the gardener.

'It's OK.,' I called back. 'It's only me.'

'Sorry, Miss,' he replied, half blinding me with his torch. 'Oi didn't know it wor you. You been out 'ave you then, Miss? It ain't right safe anymore for a young lady out alone, if you pardon me saying so.' He pulled his German shepherd dog back and told it to 'shurrup'.

I went up to the front door and, by the porch's light, rummaged around in my handbag for the door key. It was not there. Frantically, I felt in my pockets but they were empty. I'd previously planned to sneak in and run straight up to my room, but with no key...

Ah well, I thought as I rang the bell, its sonorous tones

peeling through the house, here goes! I felt more than a little apprehensive, for I knew what my family's reaction would be. A feeling of gloom began to engulf me. I knew they would chuck me out like some itinerant broom salesman; but was I emotionally prepared to be some kind of pariah, unwanted?

Granddad's butler who wheezed at inconvenient moments, gasped when he saw me, just as if I were a dilapidated specimen, as if he'd seen a ghost; he gave me an affrighted look. When I attempted to walk in, for a whistle of cold air was blowing in the hall, he stood in my way, giving me an oily smile.

'Hey Morrison, I happen to be staying here, as well you know, so come on and let me in, please.'

He turned slowly, taking his time because of the state of his corns. 'Miss Janice is here,' he quailed.

It was dad who made the first appearance. 'Who?' he asked, pointedly. 'Who? I know of no-one with that name.'

Flabbergasted, I squeezed past old Morrison and told my dad not to come out with such silly things; I wasn't some nasty imp. Mum, followed closely by cousin Sam, hurried into the large panelled hall and shook her head at me. Granddad, who'd previously been singing a lusty bass, practising for the next Sabbath service, frightening Tinker the cat, was pushed in his wheelchair by a care assistant. Icily, his eyes penetrated me. Then dropping his head in his arthritic old hands, he sobbed, 'How could she? How could she?'

Spoilt Sam covered his mouth and giggled at grandpa. Someone, I think it could have been Aunt Mag, clipped his ear and he ran off up the stairs to his room, breathing abuse as he went.

My parents were angry; Aunt Mag, a short blousy woman, disappointed.

Then the unexpected happened. The four, as one, rent

their garments, buttons calling to the floor in front of me, denoting they'd not only severed all connections with me, but that I was dead.

'Well, some rotten family you come from, Janice!' exclaimed Lois, who'd been listening intently to my story so far.

Rotten family? Really? I hadn't thought of them quite like that.

A CHALLENGE

Believers, living in the easy-going tolerance of a nominal Christian lifestyle, find it difficult to comprehend how when Jews or Moslems, for example, turn to the Lord Jesus Christ they encounter immediate fierce hostility from the strictness of the religious regime.

'If anyone would come after me, he must deny himself and take up his cross daily and follow me.' (Luke 9:23.)

CHAPTER TWO

Jogging around the family of Flowers

ON 8 June 1942, a marriage was solemnised at the Worple Road Synagogue in Wimbledon between Thomas Wiseman and Miss Jessica Ruth Flowers. They had first met at the Palaise de Dance in Merton, and a love had grown between them which surprised both families and caused not a little misgiving.

For a start, there was a disparity of fortune. Thomas' father, George Wiseman, had been a coalman—a man who died before the boy was barely eight, leaving little more than elementary comforts for his family. His widow, three sons and two daughters lived in some austerity in a working class area of the town. The Flowers, however, had made a great deal of money from brewing beer. Sir John Flowers, Jnr., my grandfather, knighted by King George VI, owned The Gables, a handsome house by the side of Wimbledon Common, and lived in some style.

There was a difference, too, in temperament; the Wisemans were, on the whole, reserved, the Flowers ardent and outspoken. Indeed, the Wisemans feared that, in his courtship with Miss Flowers, Thomas had abandoned his habitual prudence and acted with impetuosity. The Flowers for their part endured the deepest fears that Jessica's attachment would end badly, that Thomas was only after her fortune. The match was a troubling enigma. If only grandfather had wrestled away all impulses to remonstrate with his daughter, for his reservations provoked in her a storm of tears.

So it was, being the satisfied owners of their own home, within just a stone's throw of Sir John's in the Jewish area of the town, Thomas and Jessica, later to be my parents, lived in a dazzling happiness despite their differences.

To me, we seemed ordinary sort of folk who never made the front page of the Sunday newspapers, although details of our comings and goings were invariably found on the inside pages, mostly because of granddad. He was not just a beneficiary of monies from the famous Flowers brewery, but a prominent philosopher and theologian, a rabbi in an ultra-Orthodox synagogue where traditional Hebrew Judaism is based on the strict observance of the law and teaching as found in the first five books of the Old Testament.

Orthodox synagogues do not use musical instruments on Sabbaths or during Jewish festivals; instead, they have a man who is a Cantor rabbi, and granddad was the Cantor, singing with a nightmarish passion concerning the 'Holy One, blessed be He', and the sufferings of our people Israel. When I knew him he seemed very old and probably toothless, for although his voice was resonant it was oddly slurred. A big man, he, when out, wore a black fur-trimmed hat, a black knee-length coat, and his black trousers looked as if they'd had a fight with his shoes, making him appear as ancient as the century perhaps.

Granddad could speak in two languages at once! With his lips he spoke in his mother tongue of English yet, using his hands, he communicated 'Sign language'. Being bi-lingual came naturally to both him and his brother Fred for their parents John-William and Sarah Flowers were both profoundly deaf, as were uncles Jack and Edwin, along with their respective wives, Harriet and Anna. Anna had a laugh like a donkey, yet never enduring the inconvenience of hearing Fred mock her with laughter. From as far back as granddad could remember, he and Fred acted as ready interpreters to this non-hearing family.

As a result of such handicaps, it was hard for the men in the family to find regular employment. So, in an attempt to combat poverty, they clandestinely brewed beer down in the cellar of John-William's small end terraced house; the more discreet neighbours would sneak in by the Flowers' back door, normally after dark, to purchase the elicit concoction. A whole jug full never cost much more than a penny or two and all the time the demand was growing.

Sarah Flowers informed her husband that her conscience had got the better of her; no longer could she help to trade in such an underhand way and she insisted on a meeting with those in the family. After many hours of heated debate, they decided to come out and openly market their recipe. Investing almost every penny they possessed, the Flowers family were soon showing a healthy profit. By 1880 they were able to increase their production and several larger business premises were obtained. They always treated their staff and families generously. Everyone was happy.

The rapidly acquired wealth of John-William and Sarah Flowers soon provided a privileged education for their sons, first at a public school in Westminster, and then at Oxford's academic seat of learning.

In 1914, whilst still fairly young, John and Fred were called up into the army and later transferred into The Royal Flying Corps. They began to experience, first hand, the horrors of the First World War.

John, a commissioned officer, was completely in the thick of the most bloody of battles and he vowed that, if he was spared until peacetime, he would serve the Lord God.

With peace restored in 1918, he took steps to free himself from being just a nominal Anglican and converted to Judaism—the reason why remaining a mystery. One year later, he began as a rabbinic student, so attempting to devote his life to God, as he'd promised.

It was about this time that granddad's mother's sister and his wealthy aunt, Kate Mann, the sole owner of Mann Breweries, made an unbeatable offer to buy out Flowers. The Flowers family tried to resist a take-over by amalgamating with Hamilton's Beers; but the Hamilton's were in financial difficulties and so were no longer a safe bet. In 1924 Mann joined forces with Crossman Brewery and 'Mann and Crossman' bought out Flowers, yet allowing them to still trade under their name—the name of Flowers lived on, bringing an unexpected sense of relief to the family.

In 1925 my great grandparents, John-William and Sarah, died within months of each other. John, the eldest son and their favourite, was left £4,250, a mighty fortune in the mid-twenties, but Fred, for some reason, seen as a waster, only inherited £1,700.

Fred Flowers snatched his cash and emigrated to Canada where he married May Richardson. The couple, after the birth of their son, Anthony, contemplated buying a chain of launderettes.

'We shall start up here in Toronto and then expand across into every city... oh, May, just think, we'll be rich!' he exclaimed.

May, a small but strong-willed woman did think and opposed her husband, considering that they should invest in the Canadian railway. Her hunch paid off and they became wealthier than any brewer back home.

In the meantime, John Flowers, a man of wealth, purchased Wimbledon's Mulberry Court—a large mock Tudor style house. Roses clad the ancient walls, with a mélange of pinks bleeding from the palest blush to the deepest crimson, all with intoxicating scents, and all hidden behind mellow high stone walls.

A widower, granddad desperately missed his wife. She was named Esther, but everyone who knew her well called her Polly. He met her when during one of his famous lecture tours, combining it with a short holiday in Dublin. Never having been out of Ireland, she was a pretty young Jewish lass with a mop of dark-brown curly hair.

As soon as he saw her large ebony eyes it was love at first sight—there would be no other woman for him. To await her correspondence seemed tiresome; he'd receive her letters with shaking fingers and a thudding heart, missing her more than he could express. Never one for anything but the briefest of formalities, granddad came straight to the point and asked her father for his daughter's hand in marriage, promising not only generous sentiments but his shares in the Flowers' fortune as well, sustaining comforts all her days.

Following her fairy-tale wedding in January 1919, Polly found herself surrounded by so many servants, all sustaining the elegant life of Mulberry Court; but the domestic arrangements rarely intruded into granddad's life, he regarding that department as much Polly's as her confinements.

Exactly nine months after their honeymoon Polly prided herself on producing a healthy boy named Jack. All too soon her physician informed her she would have another child the following Spring. After a third and fourth confinement a tiny little scrap named Jessica, my mother, came into the world. My grandparents were to have ten live children in all.

Jessica was a pale-faced sickly child with solemn eyes, much too large for her delicate face. Invariably granddad lost patience with Polly for mollycoddling her. 'You pander too much to that child,' he'd say with a tiresome regularity, feeling an intrinsic desire to turn back the clock, half regretting her birth. 'You'll make her neurotic!'

Jess's fourteen year old weaknesses reached the ears of Kate Mann's born-again Christian cousin, Nell, and her heart went out to the teenager. A prim and proper spinster who vowed she'd only have dealings with Kate's brewery when hell became frozen over, she lived in a very elegant house in Islington, a French maid attending her. A courtier, as well as being a dress designer for the rich and famous, not excluding royalty, Nell seemed to have more money than she knew what to do with.

One summer's day a black cab drew to a halt on the wide pebbled driveway. Not expecting anyone, Polly glanced out from behind the cream lacy curtains and took a sharp intake of breath. Recognition parted her lips, exclaiming it was Miss Mann! Nell was surveying the front facade as if she was contemplating buying the place. Joseph, the youngest and most mischievous of the sons, was banished to his room. Ada, the chunky old cook was ordered to cease what she was baking and, on only the finest of their crockery, to make dainty little sandwiches without the crusts.

'I have come here to make a serious offer to both you and John, Polly,' she began. 'I'll come straight to the point, for I have a cabby waiting. My proposition concerns that dear girl of yours, young Jessica.'

'Jess?' quizzed granddad. 'What about her?'

'I'd like to adopt her.'

Polly's mouth fell into a gape. 'Adopt her?' she spluttered, aghast. 'Adopt Jess?... adopt our young daughter? Have you taken leave of your senses, Nell?' Polly found herself unable to move, as if she was paralysed. She sat staring blankly, chills swept through her.

The visitor stiffened for a few seconds, sitting up even straighter on the overstuffed sofa and swallowed a cucumber sandwich. 'I have never... never had the good fortune to marry and have children of my own—and by the way, where is Jess? I'd like to see her before I go.'

'Never mind where she is. It's horrendous... there are

no words to describe... some things, some folk are really hard to take and right now, Nell, you are one of them. How dare you?'

Nell attempted to ignore Polly's remarks, although she felt the heat flooding her face. 'It's just that you and John have had more than your fair share of children, ten in all, and I have had none. I believe that if I had Jessica I could bring her up as a good Christian and train her in my profession. Just imagine. Maybe I should give you more time to consider.'

Granddad stood with his back to the big, old-fashioned fireplace and hearth, stacked with logs for the next winter, and sucked on his Sherlock Holmes type pipe. Overlooking Nell's remarks about Christianity, he thought it was a spiffing idea and, touched by her thoughtfulness, thanked her; but Polly's hot Irish temper came to the fore and, hardly your bead-cap and bonnet person, she hissed at John, and then turned on a shocked Nell, who almost fainted and needed to be revived with smelling salts.

Sighing under her breath, Nell left the house, trying to set aside her worries about Jess. She was helpless, there was nothing she could do except pray for the young girl.

In 1938, at the age of fifteen and a half, Jessica inherited from the old Flowers family the vast sum of £50; once again, a small fortune for those days. From it, she tells, she bought a new dress for her mother, along with a whole new wardrobe of clothing for herself. She had enough left for a holiday in Brighton. It was Jess's first holiday to the coast, her first breath of sea air which bucked her up no end.

Polly Flowers died from ovarian cancer at the age of forty-five in 1945—a year prior to my birth. Her death, totally unexpected, was a blow to the whole family, but a terrible shock to her doting husband and, for a year or two, he almost became a recluse, claiming he just wanted a bit of peace and quiet. However, one person didn't leave him be and that was Jim, granddad's barber. Jim was a member of the Christian Brethren and he was not slow in speaking of his faith. He held the view that everyone, including the Jews, needed to hear of God's salvation in Christ. He used every opportunity to tell Sir John that Jesus was indeed the true Messiah. Through Jim's witness granddad accepted the Lord as his Saviour only weeks before his death in 1964.

MEDITATION

Hear, O Israel: The LORD our God is one LORD; and you shall love the LORD your God with all your heart, and with all your soul, and with all your might (Deuteronomy 6:4,5, RSV).

CHAPTER THREE

The Nazi Menace

IN 1939, when Thomas Wiseman, my father, was twenty, he received his call-up papers to serve in the army. He was ordered to report to a training unit based in the old historic city of Winchester.

As part of his basic military training he, along with the other raw recruits, was marched, sometimes at the double, past the dominating statue of Alfred the Great in Broadway, over Bridge Street and up and down Magdalen Hill; all this to lick them into shape as England's fighting men.

'Platoon... wait fer it... platoon attenshun! Right turn... qui-eek march,' yelled the Drill Sergeant, his shoulders jerking downwards every time he bellowed yet another command. 'Swing those arms and get into step, Wiseman! Left, right...'

Silently, King Alfred, founder of the English nation, stood with sword lifted high, his shield by his side, and looked down on those men who, like himself eleven hundred years before, were prepared to defend this green and pleasant land from its enemies.

King Alfred was not the only observer of all this military activity. Jessica Flowers, hearing that her sweetheart, Tom, was in Winchester, immediately decided to holiday there for a week or two so she could share with him whatever off-duty hours he was allowed.

Sitting alone on a park bench, in the shadow of Alfred's statue, she saw it all.

Not one to suffer in silence, Jessica observed the strenuous activity and verbal abuse that her love endured at the hands of the non-commissioned officers and decided to take the matter further.

As the Commanding Officer opened his mail he must have roared with laughter at the letter of protest he received from Jessica, who reminded him that she was a person not without influence.

Tom's lot did not noticeably improve!

Before being posted overseas, he married my mum. The wedding was a triumph, with many saying it was the best wartime occasion they'd attended.

Father requested leave for the wedding but, at the last moment, all leave was refused, so he went AWOL from His Majesty's Forces. Neither mum, nor any of the guests knew about his misdemeanour. The shock was to come later.

Wartime prevented the newlyweds from travelling to exotic places for their honeymoon; they had to be content with borrowing Uncle Joe's flat in Wimbledon for a while, but for a much shorter time than planned. At four-thirty a.m. their sleep was disturbed by the thud thud thud of heavy army boots marching up the uncarpeted stairs. Unceremoniously, the military police, with their peaked caps pulled down low over their eyes, burst through the bedroom door and loudly ordered my half-naked dad onto his feet. The bewildered young bride, clutching the bedclothes to herself, was left behind as he was whisked away at a sharp pace to a detention centre for military offenders, otherwise known as the 'glass house' where, among other punishments, he was made to whitewash sacks of coal.

The regimental sergeant-major, chest well out, cap pulled down, stood before my dad and eyed him up and down. 'Nah then, what 'ave we 'ere then?' he asked in a loud voice.

'Private Wiseman,' replied my father.

'Private Wiseman, SIR!' corrected the RSM in a parade ground shout. 'When you speak to me, you dozy little man, you address me as SIR, do you 'ear me? I said, "do you 'ear me?" First we get 'Itler... then what do we get? We get you... you 'orrible specimen of 'umanity!'

When dad was asked his religion, the loud RSM looked up and down one of his umpteen lists before eyeing my father again. He shook his head. 'We 'ave no provision fer Jews 'ere, no kosher grub, no rabbis, no synagogues; from now on, son, you are Church of England!'

My father stammered in protest, but the RSM would have none of it—any complaints should be addressed to him in triplicate, which meant they would most likely be ignored.

Active service followed. Dad was posted overseas to join the 8th Army in the desert campaign in North Africa. At the end of 1942 he was captured by the Germans and then the Nazi nightmare followed.

When his captors at the prisoner of war camp realised he was Jewish, arrangements were immediately made to send him to a concentration camp. As he arrived in enemy occupied Europe, he was bundled with many more prisoners into a filthy, overcrowded railway wagon. There was a sense of terror in their hearts as the train, in total blackout, rumbled through the night.

The train finally screeched to a halt at its destination and he was shoved by the butt of a German rifle out on to the platform: Auschwitz.

At the death camp dad was stripped of his clothes and issued with prison garb and one thin grey blanket; like nearly all others he acquired more clothing only when another prisoner died. On one occasion he found some grass which had grown in the mud. He ate it quickly before anyone else had the chance. During his time, he witnessed people being shot, gassed, or starved to death. Disease claimed many lives—usually the elderly and the infants were the first to go. Rats, fleas and leeches almost constantly plagued the living. He often thought of escape, but it was never more than a thought. Some guards were recruited from among the Jewish prisoners who, in order to survive themselves, played a strong part in the destruction of their own people. The interns hated those Jewish traitors even more than they despised the German guards.

When dad first arrived at Auschwitz one of the older captives was helping with the disembarkation. 'Say you have a trade,' he whispered to him.

'But I haven't,' muttered dad, with a furrowed brow.

'You 'ave now, mate!' he exclaimed, giving him a gentle shove. 'You're a cobbler with me. OK?'

This helpful employment played a part in keeping dad going, for those without a trade were invariably the earliest to be herded to the gas chambers.

On the 27th of January 1945, a day when, near total collapse, dad heard a loud commotion. All the German guards appeared scared stiff. He couldn't understand what was happening. Fearlessly, groups of Jewish prisoners were dropping to their knees, openly blessing God, behaviour previously punishable by death.

The Russian army had arrived! His ordeal was over.

When the camp was liberated, dad was sent to a British military base in North Wales where he was nursed back to health.

One day there was an unexpected rapping on the front door of our home. Then, whoever it was just kept their finger on the bell...

'Who on earth could that be?' queried my mother, hurrying through the hall, beating the butler to it.

As she opened the door her ebony dark eyes widened; she gasped, her hand covering her mouth. Dad stood there with his skinny arms outstretched. Without a moment's thought, she threw her arms around him, unable to let him go, tears of joy running down her cheeks. All that mattered to them both was that they were together again—for ever.

I was born in 1946, my brother David eight years later in 1954.

The whole family celebrated and congratulated my parents on having a son. David's birth and circumcision were truly marked occasions.

He was circumcised by the Mohel—a specially trained rabbi.

I remember when the Mohel arrived; all the men followed him into the main living room, dad carrying the little baby, whilst the women waited outside in the drawing room.

Mum jumped as she heard the shrill screams of the baby, helpless to comfort him. Still tired from the birth, she buried her head in her lap, covering her ears. One of her sisters-in-law tried to comfort her, but mum just shook her off.

The door slowly creaked open. There was the Mohel holding out baby David. She quickly took hold of him, her precious little bundle and sat rocking him to and fro until the high pitched cries turned to just a snuffly whimper.

'Is it not God's blessing that you have such a fine, healthy son m'dear?' asked the Mohel in a strong Yiddish accent.

She just nodded, smiling through the blur of her tears.

Eight years later she rocked backwards and forwards, but she was in dad's arms. They sat together as if in a daze as the paediatrician at Great Ormond Street Children's Hospital approached them. 'I am afraid we could do no more for David. The Hodgkin's Disease was just too advanced. I really am so very sorry,' he said.

David was dead. Dead! They could not believe what they were hearing.

My parents never seemed to recover from the death of my little brother. Their grief was like an open ulcer that would not heal.

MEDITATION

For the love of God is broader
Than the measures of man's mind;
And the heart of the Eternal
Is most wonderfully kind.

But we make his love too narrow
By false limits of our own;
And we magnify his strictness
With a zeal he will not own.

Frederick William Faber

CHAPTER FOUR

The Best Days of Your Life?

CAROL Smillie recently interviewed the comedian Jimmy Tarbuck as her guest on the BBC television 'Smillie's People'. Far from being one of my favourite television characters, I nevertheless pricked up my ears as he recollected how one particular schoolteacher constantly made his life a misery. Even when a young Jimmy did excel in a subject the master derived pleasure in reminding him of all his failures. Glued by the memories, Mr. Tarbuck had obviously carried such hurts from his childhood and through into middle age.

Feeling an empathy, I remembered suffering at the hands of a similar person for two agonising years back in the middle fifties.

At about the age of three I started as an outpatient at Moorfields Eye Hospital in an attempt to correct a squint. Week after week I saw Mr. Cross, an eminent eye surgeon, although the consultations were getting me nowhere. Grandfather, who had little or no medical knowledge, decided he'd had enough airy-fairy theories and went to see the Consultant himself.

'I am Sir John Flowers,' he began. 'I'm sure you've heard of me...'

Rather than confess his ignorance, Mr. Cross nodded.

'Well, I want something done about my grand-daughter's sight... but if it's a question of money... no problem, just name the amount...'

I was admitted the following week for surgery on one eye and, some two or three years later, the other eye was operated on.

Those were comparatively unenlightened days when any form of hospitalisation separated babies and children from any relatives or friends who might visit.

Scared stiff, I was undressed and lifted into a bed where cot sides were in situ, as if I were a baby. Nothing having been explained to me, I returned from the operating theatre with my eye covered, the patch held in place by crêpe bandages around my head. There was no-one to kiss me goodnight, say my prayers with me, or read me a story from one of my favourite books, just one very gruff nurse who spanked me on my leg for not being able to swallow my tablets in one go.

I can remember those awful days when my sight was either blurred or I had double vision. Ophthalmic surgery was nothing like as advanced as today.

My teacher was the compassionate Mrs. Hughes who made allowances for me, moving me nearer the front, enabling me to see the blackboard without difficulty, constantly spurring me on with the delights of learning.

During the following academic year I found myself in All Saints' Junior School where Miss Smith (not her real name) was my teacher.

'Find yourself a seat,' she said, confronting the jumble of young faces on the first day of term. 'Come on, hurry up, the lot of you.'

I attempted to sit at the front, but the overbearing Joyce and her faithful lap-dog, Judith, had hogged those seats and I was left standing, searching for an empty desk nearer to the blackboard.

Miss Smith sighed. 'What's the matter with you?' she enquired in her penetratingly abrupt voice. 'Yes... yes, you girl... you with the glasses.'

I'd never been addressed as the girl with the glasses before. I scowled, for she had glasses—hexagonal rimless ones. I longed to say something in retaliation, but I had been taught always to be polite. Teachers, policemen, parents, in fact towards all grown-ups, I had to be courteous.

'I'm sorry, Miss, but I need to be at the front,' I replied, nervously. 'I can't see...'

'Well tough. There are seats at the back... go on. So, go on then—don't just stand there like a lemon.'

'Couldn't someone just change seats with me, please?'

She turned to those rooted at the front. 'Do any of you want to change with her?'

Not one child moved. Then Judith began to vacate her seat, but Joyce yanked at her sleeve and she sat down.

'Well, little Miss Specky Four Eyes, it looks as if you are remaining at the back, doesn't it?'

Several children chuckled at the insulting name she had for me, especially Joyce, the tall, plump girl who bullied anyone weaker.

'I beg your pardon, but my name is Janice, Janice Wiseman, nothing else; not "Miss Specky Four Eyes".'

An irritated Miss Smith, probably only in her early to middle twenties, soon to be married to a Scot, turned red in the face. She hadn't bargained on this response—not from me.

Previously I had excelled at school, never lower than the top two or three, but now I was failing miserably. I could not see what had been chalked up on the blackboard, so, eventually, I just didn't bother.

'You, come out here,' shot Miss Smith. 'Come out here right now, you stupid girl.'

Fearfully, I trotted out to her desk. She picked up a twelve-inch wooden ruler and hit my bare forearm until the weapon snapped in two. 'That's for looking out of the window instead of working,' she smirked, pleased to have administered the punishment. 'Now go back to your desk and pay attention in future. Do you hear? You're a dense, useless girl and someone like you will never get to be anything more than some sort of a factory girl… if that.'

Mr. Baxter was made aware of my lack of commitment concerning the schoolwork. 'All she does is stare out of the window,' he explained to my worried father. 'Maybe you should think about sending her to a special school for the not-very-bright.'

Dad shook his head. 'But she used to do so well…'

That evening dad sat me down and asked why I no longer took any interest at school. In between choking sobs, I explained. It was one of the rare occasions when he boiled over with rage.

The next day he and my mother, supported by Sir John, my granddad, a strong willed man who loved me to bits, warned the teacher concerning her actions. For a short time, running into a couple of weeks, Miss Smith changed her attitude, but it didn't last. She was soon back to her old self, hitting me with the ruler as often as possible.

When I told my grandfather things were worsening, he and my parents made the decision to transfer me to a Roman Catholic girls' fee paying school, well known for its high standards in both academic and sporting spheres. A boarding school in the heart of the Surrey countryside, it was run by a teaching order of nuns.

The Roman Catholic pupils found it a bit odd to have a Jewess in their midst and a couple occasionally called after me, 'You killed Jesus! You killed Jesus!'

I'd previously developed stomach pains and headaches, obviously manifestations of my distress and symptoms of the inward isolation and loneliness. A young postulate, aware of my past, linked me with another more sympathetic pupil and suddenly I had a friend. I began to regain my confidence and others became much more interested in me as a person. Now my battle was half over. No longer were my eyes glazed and dull, but bright and laughing. I was now happily living in a world full of interest and colour. No longer was I retreating from my environment; I was advancing to meet it.

Academically, I was doing well again. I enjoyed every subject with the exception of the religious studies. Judaism and Roman Catholicism, although the two should have complimented each other, seemed to pull in opposite directions, and I didn't like it. So, when I was not quite thirteen I decided to give up all religious observance. After all, I thought, there are many Jews who are not religious but who are still very aware of their Jewish roots; lots of Jewish people do not fulfil their duties to the letter of the law, so I will not fulfil mine.

On voicing my decision, first to Reverend Mother and then to my family, mum suggested I should become a weekly boarder so that I'd be home for Sabbaths. Religious observances and family life were very important to my parents and these two factors, it was felt, needed to be instilled into me before it was too late. Therefore, every Friday father collected me from school and drove me home.

Rain or shine, dad was so full of the joys of life that his bursting high spirits had to find some outlet and singing was the natural thing. 'I wonder who's kissing her now,' he'd wholeheartedly let rip at full volume. Then he would take long breaths and sing, 'She'll be coming round the mountain when she comes—yes, she'll be coming round the mountain when she comes, coming round the mountain…' utterly at peace with the world, chuckling with immense satisfaction. I found him an embarrassment!

Once home I was obliged to share in the Jewish Sabbath, whether I wanted to or not! The family expected it of me.

A short time before sunset on the Friday, the Sabbath,

called in Hebrew the *Shabbat,* is welcomed in by the woman of the house lighting two candles. In our home my mother performed this task, although, sometimes, she would encourage me to also light a candle.

In Orthodox homes, such as ours, men celebrate the start of the Sabbath in the synagogue with a service.

Just before the eating of the meal, all Jews perform a ceremony called *Kiddush*. This involves blessing and drinking wine (a symbol of joy), and blessing the day itself. Father, according to tradition, would praise my mother and bless my brother and me, along with any other children who might be visiting the house.

The actual meal began with a blessing of bread. There were always two loaves called *Hallot,* made in a special braided way. During each course *Shabbat* songs are sung, and the meal ends with thanksgiving.

My mother always looked tired by the time the Sabbath was over. Although no work is done on the Sabbath itself, there was always plenty of work to be done in the preparation for it, such as shopping, cooking and preparing the Shabbat table. All the food to be eaten was cooked beforehand and kept warm on a low heat. In Orthodox homes cooking, or lighting the gas, or switching on the electricity, is forbidden. So Friday, before sunset, is a busy day.

Every Friday, over the meal, granddad would remind us, ad nauseam, what a special day it was, and how the Sabbath was linked to the creation of the world. He pointed out that according to the story in the Book of Genesis, God made the world in six days, and on the seventh day he rested and was refreshed.

'Now listen!' he would say, '*Shabbat* is a day of worship, study of the law, and leisure. Nothing else. Don't you dare forget that.'

The close of the Sabbath was marked by yet another

ceremony. Wine was used again, and this time a braided candle with several wicks was lit. A spice box containing sweet smelling spices was displayed and the final act was to pour the wine over the candle to put it out. Everyone present would wish each other a good week.

My week began again on the Sunday afternoon when I returned to the Convent school in time for tea, which always consisted of hot buttered toast, home made strawberry jam and mugs of steaming hot tea.

MEDITATION

Is there no balm in Gilead; is there no physician there? Why then is not the health of the daughter of my people recovered? (Jeremiah 8:22, AV)

CHAPTER FIVE

Where are you God?

AFTER about two years of being a weekly boarder I began to meet up on a Saturday evening with a teenage group. Many of us, all Jewish, had been chums for years as most of our parents were friends too, mainly through the religious services and social events that took place in and around the synagogue.

We teenagers usually met up in the Orinoco coffee bar and we would chat for what seemed ages over a cup of frothy, expresso coffee, discussing evocative subjects such as politics and religion.

Constantly confused concerning the existence of God, I would listen carefully as to what the others in the group had to say about a Supreme Being. After a while, I secretly tried to please him, if he existed at all, by attempting to measure up to the standards set by the Ten Commandments. The religious guideposts made morality a fairly uncomplicated business, as they clearly assessed my conduct as either good or bad. Surely, if I lived a good life then this so-called God might reveal himself to me.

Sin, I understood, was a failure to live up to the standard, but the way some Roman Catholics handled their moral failures differed greatly from the way I had to cope. They did not all seem to take failure too seriously but went to the confessional, got it off their chests and carried on much as before. The Day of Atonement, which takes place in the autumn of each year, is when we Jews repent of our sins and seek forgiveness. However, in my case I seemed to repress my guilt and constantly carry it about with me.

I did wonder if God might be found in other religions, but this idea was most certainly discouraged by my family, for in those days, people were not encouraged to investigate other faiths. One of the nuns who taught religion to the girls in our class warned them against investigating Judaism. She said if they did it would be a horrible sin; appropriate punishments would follow. My friend, Susan, did make some comment about Jesus, Mary and Joseph being of my Jewish religion, and she was sent to the Mistress of Discipline and silenced.

'You ought to be searching for God in our own religion,' stated my Uncle Joe. 'Judaism has a great deal to offer. You don't have to switch from our beliefs to something else to find spiritual fulfilment.'

Chatting with some upper sixth formers, who were obviously more sophisticated than the girls in my age group, I noticed they seemed to be moving away from the religion of their childhood. Some had travelled to exotic places, seen other cultures and acquired a tolerance for other people's customs. They had begun to explore their own sexuality in a less puritanical way and were throwing off the constraints of their religious upbringing. What they had to say was fascinating, yet of no real help in my search for God.

Sometimes I felt very Jewish; at other times I felt myself to be something else. What I was sure of was my need to find something or someone to believe in. I felt that there must be a Power behind the universe; there must be a meaning for my life here on earth and beyond into eternity. If there was anyone up there then why didn't he manifest himself to me?

Strolling through the school's garden, I picked a rose. I stood fingering the soft pink petals, concluding that man, not even the finest of scientists, could make such a lovely thing. The God whom I was seeking must be responsible for creation.

Later that afternoon, just after tea, I wandered into the Convent's little chapel. There was a smell of stale incense pervading the place. Staring up at the plain wooden cross hanging above the altar, I breathed, 'Oh, where are you, God? Where are you? If you really do exist then here I am. Please make yourself known to me.'

One of the Irish nuns drifted almost silently into the chapel and was surprised to find me, of all people, praying. After genuflecting, she sat close beside me, too close. I felt irritated.

'Can I help?' she asked. I shook my head.

'Seeing you here, my girl, I was just thinking how you'd make a lovely Catholic, to be sure,' she whispered, giving me a nudge. 'That is, if you weren't Jewish...'

I turned my head away and sighed. Taking the hint she went to the back of the chapel to tidy up a pile of hymnbooks. She gave a bob and left.

Alone again, my mind returned to the all-important issue of God's existence. If there was no God, then what hope did I have?

Two of us were at the back of the English class reading forbidden selections from D. H. Lawrence's *Lady Chatterley's Lover.*

The woman in charge of our class was both a student and a Protestant. (The Teachers' Training College allocated her to the Convent through some administrative error; the following week she was to be transferred to school in Cheam for her teaching practice.)

'You... what is your name?'

'Janice.'

'Well, Janice, bring out what are you doing?'

I was approaching sixteen, yet I felt as if she was

treating me like a junior, as if I was in Miss Smith's class all over again.

'Janice. Did you not hear me the first time?'

'Yes, miss,' I sighed.

My eyes slanted towards Wendy, my classmate, as if to question what I should do.

'Quick, quick, she's religious,' Wendy whispered from behind her desk lid. 'Take her out this Bible—tell her you were reading from it.'

'I can't,' I said, shaking my head. 'I might get found out.'

'Janice,' exclaimed the student, 'I presume you'll be coming out here to me today, eh?'

'Who on earth does she think she is?' muttered Wendy, thrusting her Catholic Bible into my hand and giving me a shove.

'Mother Superior!' I giggled back.

I wandered forward with the Bible, half turning once to glance back at my supporter.

'I... er...I was reading from this, miss,' I smirked. 'This... this Bible.'

The student teacher raised one eyebrow in disbelief. 'So from which part of this Bible were you reading?' she enquired, staring hard at me, drumming her fingers on the desk.

I shrugged.

'When you have decided what you were reading, let me know—and before prep, do you hear?'

I shook my head defiantly.

'Oh, but you will,' came her sharp reply.

I sloped off back to my seat, all the time muttering under my breath what I thought of her.

Rather than be put in detention, during prep I went to see the student. 'I wasn't reading from the Bible. I lied to you.'

She sat back down and signalled for me to do the same. 'Do you ever read the Bible, Janice?'

I told her, 'No.'

'Would you like to come to Westminster Chapel this Sunday?' she asked, and then continued, 'I've been in membership there since becoming a Christian six months ago. Dr. Martyn Lloyd-Jones is the minister. He's a famous preacher with a remarkable ministry... he's an exceptional expositor of the Word of God—thousands come to hear him.'

I shrugged. At that stage I couldn't have cared less about her minister, yet I wondered what she'd meant by 'becoming a Christian'. It seemed an odd remark and I'd never heard the nuns speak in such a way. I thought that to become a Christian meant one had to be christened in the Catholic Church.

The student was persistent, if nothing else, as she asked why I wouldn't want to go to church.

'I'm Jewish.'

'That's all right, Janice. Please just ask your parents if you can come on Sunday. I'm sure you'd enjoy it.'

I was sure I wouldn't.

During the following Sabbath the time seemed to drag for me, so I decided I'd liven up the occasion. Remembering the student teacher's invitation, I brought up about attending Westminster Chapel.

'My life. You want to do *what?*' boomed grandfather. 'A church... a Christian church? Over my dead body!'

Mother hurried back into the room. 'Why are you upsetting granddad?' she questioned.

'I only said I wanted to go to Westminster Chapel, that's all.'

'What do you mean "that's all"?'

Granddad rocked backwards and forwards in his chair. 'Mark my words, this girl will bring disgrace upon Israel.

And someone of Abraham's seed, too!' muttered the old rabbi.

'Be quiet, Dad!' my mother snapped.

'Are you mad?' my father asked me. 'Jews don't go to Church. Never...'

Mother shushed at both the men, determined that *she* would settle the matter with me.

'Have you taken leave of your senses? I'm telling you, no one else, but me. I'm telling you that you're *not* going,' she yelled. 'Listen to me, Jan. Janice, you are a Jewish girl... you're not going and that's the end of the matter. I don't want to hear another thing about Christian churches. OK?'

So I went.

FOR OUR MEDITATION

From one man he made every nation of men, that they should inhabit the whole earth... God did this so that men would seek him and perhaps reach out for him and find him, though he is not far from each one of us. (Acts 17:26,27.)

You will seek me and find me when you seek me with all your heart. I will be found by you, declares the LORD, and I will bring you back from captivity. (Jeremiah 29:13,14.)

CHAPTER SIX

The Invitation

I HURRIED to meet Betsy, the student teacher, outside London's Victoria Railway Station. I was early, twenty minutes early, and I had to hang around as the fine drizzle was falling and the whole of London seemed cloaked with crystal-tipped gloom. When she arrived, neat and respectable, we strode jauntily through Stag Place and along to Westminster Chapel.

As I sat with her up in the balcony, directly facing the pulpit, I wondered how on earth two thousand people could sit motionless, in complete silence, with all eyes glued on the Welshman in the Geneva gown as he stood to preach with an authority everyone seemed to accept. All this was in stark contrast to our synagogue worship where one is free to move around at will and chat.

When the service was over, the length of which came as quite a shock to me, those staying for the day scurried off to rescue their jacket potatoes from the church's ovens, for every Sunday a basic lunch was consumed on the premises. The conversation along the trestle tables was mostly about the hour's sermon. Feeling like a spare part, I sat examining a crease in the tablecloth, trying to appear as bright as those around me, all skilfully untangling Christian knots with their Biblical knowledge.

Filled with a momentary wave of dismay, I had not realised when I accepted Betsy's invitation that it was to be a full day's programme! After the lunch, which was nothing like my mother's Sunday roasts, Betsy and her friends took a circular walk around St. James' Park, with me trailing, before assembling with the other women in one of the church rooms for a Bible study. Most of the women, of indeterminate years, seemed to me very old, as did most people over thirty! Only Betsy was younger.

Tea and sandwiches followed. A prayer meeting led up to the evening service, which for me, as an unimpressed non-Christian teenager, was no better than the morning act of worship. This proceeded a time of fellowship when those people whom I regarded as awful and congenitally incapable of doing anything wrong, stood around in groups, drinking coffee and talking about such things as when they were born again. All this left me even more like the proverbial fish out of water, very much the awkward pupil of the serious teacher with the still face. I could not see what all the fuss was about, catapulting me into a further state of religious doubt. I was jolly glad to be on my way home.

'Well, Janice, I suppose you loved every moment of being with that teacher woman, eh?' asked my dad from behind his Sunday newspaper. He was a man of temperate, even indifferent, belief himself and he deplored any fervent expression in me. On the whole he enjoyed synagogue life, but he had not grown into it because of any overwhelming religious conviction.

Gathering myself into a puffed-up self-importance, I stood as upright as a plaster Madonna in the convent where I'd attended school. 'Yes,' I said, not prepared to admit defeat. 'It was absolutely great and I'm going again next week!'

Grandfather was what you might call an old fashioned kind of rabbi; he sat in our house praying with a rocking motion that I would not bring dishonour upon Israel, but my mother snapped at him, telling him to shut up.

I repeated the morning services, lunches, walks, Bible studies, teas, evening worship and the fellowship times for Sunday after Sunday. My Jewish parents suspected that I was only going to Westminster Chapel out of sheer rebellion, although they worried that the place was a seedbed for unhealthy fanaticism. However, my new found Christian friends were encouraged by my regular attendance at the Chapel, believing I was getting keen; although I was now inwardly resisting most of the fellowship groups on the grounds that such things were the thin edge of the wedge.

There was, however, a younger element in Westminster known as the 'Chapel children', as well as myself and some other teenage waifs and strays. I cannot speak for the others, but I found it a pleasure and a delight to get away from the 'ancients', and attend the young people's discussion class. This was under the leadership of Fred (later Sir Fred) Catherwood—it was nicknamed 'Fred's Class'—a committed group with a spiritual impact. It was through his interpretation of Scripture that I was beginning to see that first glimmer of light and I quite liked what I saw and heard, of what it truly meant to be a Christian. All this was starting to make sense.

Nevertheless, I had a stumbling block; sadly, the zealous Betsy, whom I now regarded as like a pushy insurance person. She kept telling me that I was nothing but a wretched sinner and that I should flee from the wrath to come. She only told me about hell and I began to feel enraged. With a tremendous sense of relief, I decided one Sunday evening that enough was enough. I made up my mind there and then that I would never attend Westminster Chapel again—or any church, come to that! As for the synagogue, I would not commit an act of sabotage; I'd only go along if there were a Bar Mitzvah, a wedding, or a bit of a do.

This being my last evening service, I determined to pass the time by reading from a Bible which someone had left behind on the ledge in front of me. After all, it had to be preferable to counting the large organ pipes, or the men's balding heads! I picked it up in a slow quiet way so I'd not disturb the rest of the congregation, all hanging onto Dr Lloyd-Jones' every word. Flicking through the pages at random, it opened at Isaiah, chapter 53. Knowing only a little Old Testament scripture, I remembered a rabbi once preaching from this passage. He said it referred only to the suffering servant Israel; it had nothing to do with Jesus. I wondered, as I read through the chapter, whether or not he'd been mistaken, for maybe this was indeed about the Messiah. The Christians claimed that Jesus was the Messiah. They said he was the Holy One of Israel. They wholeheartedly believed he was their Messiah too,—their Christ, the Anointed One who had fulfilled all the Old Testament Scriptures.

'Who has believed our message?' verse one asked.

'But why should I, Lord? I'm a well-bred kind of girl, from a good family, public school, clearly knowing all the right people.' It was ridiculous to worry out of hand that I was bad, yet I still felt no better, just full of murky gloom, like a lesser mortal valiantly struggling not to wilt. Knowing I was an unbeliever, a momentary wave of terror was borne in upon me; I suddenly wanted to trust him, to commit myself to him.

Without more ado I read on further until I had completed the entire chapter. Then I began to read it over again, homing in on the third verse.

'He was despised and rejected by men.'

I had both despised and rejected him.

'Lord Jesus, come into my life,' I inwardly prayed, closing my eyes as tightly as I could. 'I admit I'm a sinner and I am sorry for my sins. Come in as my Saviour and cleanse me. Come in, as my Lord and Master and I will serve you all my life. Amen.'

I trusted his promise and thanked him for his Word. But then God performed a stupendous miracle. He gave me a new life for it was then, having opened my eyes, that I saw clearly the head and shoulders outline of a very bright Being. I suppose it was all over in a moment yet, during that time, oblivious of the large congregation, I reached out to touch him. The one who created the beautiful pink rose I once picked from the Convent's garden was there before me.

I'd secretly sought after God. Now my search was rewarded. At 7.22 p.m. on the 22nd of August, 1962, I moved from uncertainty to faith, from darkness to light. I knew that whatever sins I had committed were forgiven. I was born again. I had become a child of God, spiritually a new creation in Christ. My inward yearning for God was now satisfied.

FOR REFLECTION

I heard the voice of Jesus say,
'Come unto me and rest;
Lay down, thou weary one, lay down
Thy head upon my breast.'
I came to Jesus as I was,
Weary and worn and sad.
I found in Him my resting place
And He has made me glad.

I heard the voice of Jesus say,
'Behold I freely give
The living water; thirsty one,
Stoop down and drink and live.'

I came to Jesus and I drank
   Of that life-giving stream;
My thirst was quenched, my soul revived,
   And now I live in Him.

I heard the voice of Jesus say:
   'I am this dark world's Light;
Look unto me, thy morn shall rise,
   And all thy day be bright.'
I looked to Jesus, and I found
   In Him my Star, my Sun;
And in that light of life I'll walk
   Till travelling days are done.

(Horatius Bonar, 1808-89)

CHAPTER SEVEN

Farewell

HAVING spent several hours immersed in the Scriptures, St. John's Gospel in particular, I wanted to be nothing more now than a receptacle of the sleep of the just, unconscious, totally submitted to the night, yet sleep eluded me. Hoisting myself up on one elbow and squinting into the darkness, I fumbled to again switch on the small bedside lamp, immediately bathing the cosy, square bedroom into pools of dazzling brilliance. I groped for the alarm clock. Shaking the unreliable timepiece, I grimaced, breathing forcefully from behind my teeth; the wretched contraption had stopped again.

Throwing back the duvet, I slipped my feet from the warm bed shivering involuntarily, stretched across to the wicker armchair where my dressing gown, the one which flapped around my ankles when I walked, which had been lazily thrown there the night before. Parting the pink floral curtains that fell in ample folds to the floor, I gazed out into the haunting stillness of the night. At that moment the full moon made a brief appearance from behind a passing cloud, dancing in fragments through the gaps between the branches of a huge withered up old tree. It was just possible, by squinting hard, to see the local parish church's illuminated clock under indifferent stars. It was a little after one-thirty.

Mum, having paid a nocturnal trip to the loo, was immediately sensitive to my movements.

'Yoo-hoo, Janice, are you all right?' she called in a loud whisper, straining hard to catch any sound of betraying activities from within. 'Would it be OK for me to come in?'

Hypnotised by fatigue, but now agog, I reeled rapidly, almost in a stumbling orbit, back into bed, dressing gown and all, in a frightening jumble, feigning sleep.

She put her head around my door. 'Oh, sorry,' she said, crestfallen, her eyes straying in. 'I didn't mean to wake you. It's just that—well, I thought I heard you...'

Camouflaged under the bulky bedding, I faked a lazy yawn. 'Its OK. You'd better come in'.

'Hmm. I suppose you can't sleep because of this foolish decision of yours, eh,' Mum remarked, her mind knitting away with speculation, forced to no other conclusion. 'Leaving Art College... it must all be playing on your mind, just as it is on ours.'

Suddenly, she had one of her blinding flashes. 'Hey, I won't be long—I'll fetch us some camomile tea. That'll help... it makes all the difference in the world, does a nice cup of tea.'

'Mum, please, I don't want any. I really don't like it.'

Her eyes narrowed fractionally into slits as she steepled one finger. 'Of course y'do. Now I'll be back in just a jiffy,' she declared, not prepared to negotiate.

Effortlessly, like a sprinter getting off his block, she darted down the stairs to the little hall and then into the kitchen where she plugged in the kettle, dropping tea into the pot.

Sitting up in bed, chin on my chest, tightly hugging my knees under the continental quilt, I groaned aloud to a small, threadbare Teddy with only one eye—a relic of childhood and a patient confidant. I complained with an air of sheepish resolution and a sense of foreboding, how my mother's 'all girls together cuppa' would mean a long oration concerning my future; haranguing me on the foolhardiness of listening to Christians, Dorothy, Betsy's friend, in particular; of suddenly quitting Art College. Otherwise she'd most likely progress on to the 'Have you forgotten the sacrifices daddy and I made for you to go to college in the first place?' scenario, as if money was a problem to them, beneficiaries from the Flowers breweries. Oh, it was the wrong time for such weightier topics of conversation, but still mum would do as she jolly well liked.

Moments later, mum, with shuffling steps and pushing my creaking bedroom door shut with her bottom, the old lock making a resounding click, emerged with a tray of the steaming medicinal beverage.

It wasn't long before the old familiar pattern set in. 'I remember…,' began mother, with a surging ocean of vivid memories, squeezing my hand, 'I remember when I was a teenager, how I got crazy thoughts, but… oh… never, never daft ideas about Christianity.'

I sighed, taking a long swallow.

'… as I was saying, never Christianity. But, there, it'll only be a nine day wonder, just like your pop idols and that peace movement…'

Oh why couldn't she have gone back to bed, or been robbed of the power of speech? Only for a while, not forever—just for tonight.

'No, Janice, I've told your Granddad not to worry—you'll be over it all soon. We just need to be patient. You'll be back to your old self before long. Maybe you can enrol again when you are thinking straight.'

As a student on the foundation course at the Wimbledon College of Art and Design I had excelled. Part of the course was the life class. Betsy's closest friend, Dorothy, an only child of elderly parents and a spinster in her late thirties, was old for her years, maybe because of the sheltered life she had led so far. It was she who'd told me I should give up Art College. On enquiring why she—referring to the 'life' classes which were a vital part of the course—informed me I was nothing more than a budding 'pornographer'! I couldn't have been more shocked.

'What if your drawings got into the wrong hands?' she asked, with a frown. 'Your work may well encourage unhealthy thoughts... and you claiming to be a Christian, too!'

I wanted to retaliate, explaining how my work only showed line and form, light and shade. Nevertheless, I was still a very new believer, young for my seventeen years and incredibly impressionable, desperately longing to do the right thing in the sight of the Lord Jesus Christ. Believing that the older, mature Christians held in their grasp all the right answers it was to them, my spiritual props, I came. Listening to her words, instead of making up my own mind, I regrettably abandoned the College course, wanting my new found faith to grow, to be uppermost and solid.

Although during the early sixties there were still those who discouraged participation in drama, art and entertainment, there were others who questioned the rigid division of life into sacred and secular. In my Jewish cultural background, based on the Old Testament, the whole of life was seen to be important and God given. One of the Jewish rabbinic writings states, 'A man will have to give account on Judgement Day of every good thing he could have enjoyed and didn't.'

There were many in the church of those days who curtailed their activities, not because the Spirit of God had convicted them of wrongdoing, but because they were afraid of disapproval; of what their Christian friends might think of them if they ventured outside the constricted lifestyle: no theatre, no cinema, no dancing.

On the British musical scene it was not really until Cliff (now Sir Cliff) Richard, performing in show business where he took a stand as a Christian believer, that the mould began to be broken.

Even so, many evangelical churches still seemed to think artists were only there to do posters! One minister asked me to design and paint a poster which regrettably created hilarity from the congregation, but caused him and me some embarrassment, for it read:

THE MINISTER WILL BE PLEASED TO SEE ANY VISITORS TO THE CHURCH IN HIS VESTY AFTER THE SERVICE.

Suddenly, the batting of moth's wings against the window caused mum to stare up in alarm; the teapot stopped in mid-air and her eyebrows went up.

'Jan, your curtains are open. With your light on people will be able to see in,' she said. 'I'll close them for you,' she said, launching herself towards the drapes, the grim possibilities of peeping Toms racing in her imagination.

'No. No thanks. Just leave them be, please.'

Totally bewildered, she repeated herself, looking with a twinge of apprehension, comfortless around the room. 'But...' she began,somewhat mystified.

'No!' I leapt up. 'Did you not hear? I want them left. Why don't you go back to bed and leave me in peace? You treat me as if I'm a little kid— oh why...?' I asked, amidst a volley of questions.

'Right. I'll do just that,' she burst out, her lips trembling, as though she was unable to say much more.

Now I'd snapped in the kind of tone that got her back up. If only I'd held my tongue and wrestled away all impulses to remonstrate with her.

I sighed. 'No, mum, please don't go. I'm sorry,' I said in a form of unexpected contrition. Fiddling with a thread of cotton straying from the quilt's seam, I gathered my courage. 'Look, mum, I'm pretty sure I'm doing the right thing,' I said. 'I know you don't, but I'm trying to please God in a new way. Try and understand.'

She shook her head, eventually having her own way and closing the curtains. 'You should have made up your own mind—not listening to some old spinster, old enough to be your mother. That church has a lot to answer for. Perhaps dad will be able to talk some sense into you when he takes you out tomorrow. Who knows?' She plunged downwards to give me a goodnight kiss before making her way to the door. She turned and looked into my dark brown eyes. 'You're breaking our hearts, you know.'

Dad, often an easy going sort of chap, was invariably the most impatient of all people when he became any sort of a teacher, regarding his pupils as mentally subnormal low life.

I was seventeen and anxious to learn to drive. 'I'll teach you!' he had exclaimed, jumping out of his chair. 'We'll have you a driver in no time.'

Mum was unsure. When I was really quite young, maybe only about five or six, he took me along to the Latimer Road swimming pool late one Sunday morning and, when I didn't immediately turn into an Olympic gold medallist there and then, he muttered on for the rest of the day. 'If she just did exactly as I'd said… if she'd trust me… if she'd just have realised she wasn't going to drown… that the water would hold her up, that I'd hold her up!'

Oh, and then there was the bright red two wheeler bike which was much too big and heavy for me. 'If she'd just do as I told her,' he yelled. 'She has no idea of balance! She turns the handle-bars in the wrong direction and wonders why she falls of—don't blame me for the cut on her knee, for before I knew it she was in the gravel.'

And now, this very day, he planned on teaching me to drive!

'Dad', I began, a worried look across my brow, 'May I have proper lessons with a school of motoring? I think I'd do better with a real instructor.'

'An instructor! What can an instructor teach you that I can't?'

'Well, he might be a little more patient, don't you think?'

'What d'yer mean "more patient", eh? I'm *always* patient!'

I shrugged, staring in the direction of my mother, hoping for her support—but she had that distant, far away look which really said it all: it said, 'Leave me out of it.'

That morning dad marched me out and sat me behind the wheel of his old black Ford and, for about the first time ever, he was the nervous passenger in the seat where one has a different view of the road and the oncoming traffic.

After I kangarooed the car along the first few yards, dad raised his eyebrows heavenwards and signed, fingers drumming on his knee.

'Steer it straight; no, put your left foot right down on the clutch before changing gear… my life, at this rate I'll need a new gear-box! No, no, not crunching it like that… mind that bus! What do you mean "which bus"? You'll kill that cyclist if you are not more careful. Mind! look out! Slow down! That's it… that's it… that's enough! I'll drive us home.'

My mother stared at us. 'My, you're both home sooner than I'd expected,' she said with surprise.

'Home', boomed my father. 'It's a wonder we are home at all. It's a miracle we're not both in St Helier's Hospital mortuary.'

'Now, now, dear, don't exaggerate.'

'Exaggerate? I'm not exaggerating. She nearly killed a cyclist and then, when I said, "Mind the bus," do you know what she said?'

Mum shook her head, showing little or no interest.

'I'll tell you what she said—she said "what bus"? What bus indeed! How can you not see a great big red London bus in front of you? She'd be safer behind a machine gun than a wheel. Heavens, a car is just as much a lethal weapon as…'

Mum smiled in my direction and, seeing I was near to tears, gave me a bit of a hug and told him to be quiet.

'Don't tell me to be quiet. I tell you I was safer in front of Rommel's lot during the last war than I was with her today.'

'All he did was shout,' I began, attempting to get in my two pennyworth. 'I've never been in the driver's seat before and he virtually expected me to be ready for the Grand Prix. Shout, shout, shout! How can I learn anything when he's constantly yelling all the time? He makes me all of a dither.'

Dad attempted to open his mouth again, but this time it was mum who did the talking. 'If you weren't so tight-fisted you'd have *paid* for her to learn to drive,' she snapped, scowling hard at him.

'Tight-fisted! Me? Tight-fisted! that's the last thing I am—in fact, my middle name should be Money Bags!'

The next day it was mum who, with dad's money, paid for me to have twenty lessons with the British School of Motoring.

'She'll need more than twenty,' sniped dad. 'More like two hundred and twenty!'

Soon it was the big day, the day of my test. An hour before coming face to face with the examiner I had my final lesson. 'You'll do fine,' said the chap from the British School of Motoring. 'Don't be nervous—take a deep breath and drive for him as you have driven for me. OK?'

The examiner was as po-faced as I'd half expected, but that wasn't my main problem. It was dad! Everywhere I went, he followed. His car was constantly on my tail—all I saw in my mirror was his Ford. When I did the expected three point turn, he was parked a little way away, watching me, both thumbs up.

'And what do you think you were playing at, dad?' I demanded, banging through the house like a German storm-trooper. 'Why were you following me?'

'Because you were in the car with an entirely strange man, for goodness sake. How would I know whether or not you were safe?'

'He was the examiner! What harm would I have come to with him, eh? You could have unnerved me so much that I may have failed.'

'But you didn't, did you?' he beamed.

And then a thought struck him. 'I hope you don't think you are going to use my car to go swanning off up to that Westminster Church... '

'Chapel,' I corrected.

'Christian church, OK? If you insist on giving up art college and irritating us by going up there, then you can jolly well find the money to go by train.'

MEDITATION

Is my life given to the Lord for him to use, in whatever way he pleases?

Am I in the place of God's appointment and am I prepared to be disturbed by him if he has something else for me to do?

Do I live my life in compartments, or is my life an integrated whole?

CHAPTER EIGHT

Short Arms, Deep Pockets

I HADN'T quite reached eighteen and so, for the few months before I was old enough to go into nursing, I managed to acquire a temporary post in a small bookshop. The combination of being among books and meeting a variety of folk was enjoyable.

At the end of my first month I became the proud owner of a pay packet, which seemed to make the job even more worthwhile!

One Sunday I was having tea at Westminster Chapel and Margaret Padden, the wife of a deacon, sat opposite me.

'How are you getting on at work?' she asked.

'Fine, thanks. In fact, I was paid on Friday,' I replied, feeling more than a little pleased with myself. 'Money at last, eh? And all mine!'

'No, dear, it isn't all yours, you know. Ten per cent belongs to the Lord,' she explained, gently.

It was outrageous! I frowned at her in a quizzical sort of a way. 'What do you mean? How can that be?'

'If you do not give ten per cent then you'll be robbing God,' she continued. 'It is quite clear in the Scriptures. Here look...

"Will a man rob God? Yet you rob me.

But you ask, 'How do we rob you?'

In tithes and offerings...

Bring the whole tithe into the storehouse, that there may be food in my house."' (Malachi 3:8-10)

'She's right, you know, said the Rev. George Hemming, the assistant minister who had joined us at the table. 'If every Christian faithfully gave just ten per cent of their gross income then there would be "meat in the Lord's house"—in other words, the work of the Lord would not be impoverished.'

I certainly did not want to rob God. I wanted to obey him in everything, but there was still an element of rebellion within me. It was at times like this, that I would rather have had a God who was stuffed in the cupboard and only came out when I found the keys. I'd worked for my pay packet and I had plans for every penny. I needed to pay Betsy for my keep, as I could not expect her to keep me. I needed to pay for my rail fares to and from both church and my place of employment. I have always washed my hair nearly every day of my life and I was now going to buy shampoo, the best of Vidal Sassoon's. Esté Lauder perfume—the expensive kind—and deodorants, came high on my list of vital necessities. I twitted on about my many wants that would see off my salary. If there was anything left over then I would most certainly drop the odd coin in the Sunday collections.

'After all,' I reasoned, 'there were many wealthy Christians in the congregation who could not only afford to tithe, but to give love gifts as well. I couldn't.'

Month after month I gave just a little of what I earned until the time I entered nursing.

Three months after starting my training I joined the Nurses' Christian Fellowship. During one meeting the subject of 'tithing' came up.

'Don't you tithe your gross income, Janice?' asked Christine, one of the staff nurses who originated from the Isle of Skye.

I shook my head and explained that on a first year student's salary, I could not afford to tithe. 'You see, my family aren't around to help me out like the parents of some of the others do.'

'Never mind the others and their parents. You cannot afford not to.'

'Whatever do you mean?'

Christine opened her well-thumbed Bible at the book of Malachi.

'''Test me in this,' says the LORD Almighty, 'and see if I will not throw open the floodgates of heaven and pour out so much blessing that you will not have room enough for it.''' (Malachi 3:10)

'So what I'm saying, Janice,' Chris continued, 'is that if you tithe your gross income, you will never want any necessity. If you don't tithe you'll be like the janitor of some old and beautiful stately home, refusing to allow the owner to come in and live there. You'll be shutting out God.'

From that day I began to tithe. And it was true—I did not go without. In fact, I always seemed to have more than enough, enabling me to give over and above the tithe—a 'love gift', they called it.

My friend, Sue, was working with Voluntary Service Overseas in a famine area of India. Her welcome letters told of many sad and depressing problems with the exception of one particular heart-warming incident concerning a Christian believer named Sopan. This man had only the few clothes he wore and very little else. His food supply was reduced to a few cupfuls of grain and two cupfuls of rice. On an old piece of cloth Sopan spread out the grain and divided it into ten parts. A tenth was left on the old cloth. He did exactly the same with the rice. He then took his tithe and gave it to a young mother who was desperate for food to feed her child.

I never heard of Sopan again, but I've always remembered his love for the Lord and the way his tithing outshone the life-style of so many of us in the materialistic

Western world. And I had begrudged giving my tenth.

Nothing offers so practical a test of our love for Christ or for others, as does our attitude to money and possessions. However, despite what I was told in those early days of seeking to honour God in my handling of money, I began to wonder if tithing is scriptural. There is the common idea among Christians that today God asks for a tenth, but the fact remains that in the New Testament Christians are nowhere asked to tithe.

It would appear that tithing goes further back in history than many Christians realise. It existed in Babylon, Persia and Egypt. Abraham knew of its existence when he migrated from Ur of the Chaldees. It was accepted and developed as a very real part of Hebrew religious practice and, when Jacob made a covenant with God at Bethel, it included the payment of tithes:

"'This stone that I have set up as a pillar will be God's house, and of all that you give me I will give you a tenth.'" (Genesis 28:22)

Under the old covenant one tenth was for the Levites, Temple expenses, the poor, the festivals and the priesthood. The tithe did not apply only to money but to grain, animals, fowls and herbs. This practice was still observed by the Pharisees in New Testament times.

Actually, the New Testament references to tithing seem unfavourable. Consider the self-righteous Pharisee, comparing himself with others, says, "'I give a tenth of all that I get'" (Luke 18:12).

To me it seems what was commanded under the law of the Old Covenant is only a shadow of what may be expected under grace, and that to niggle about proportions and to give the Lord a mere tenth, shows a complete lack of understanding of the Christian approach to 'giving' and 'stewardship' which have a very real place in New Testament teaching.

It can be argued that those who object to giving a tenth seldom give more, and often less. Even in the Old Testament it was recognised that some of God's people were to give more than others. At the Feast of Tabernacles when the people were summoned to appear before the Lord, the Scripture says: 'Each of you must bring a gift in proportion to the way the LORD your God has blessed you' (Deuteronomy 16:17). And this appears to be the principle which has continued in the New Testament: 'And the disciples determined, every one according to his ability, to send relief unto the brethren who lived in Judea; and they did so...' (Acts 11:29 RSV).

Paul's instructions to the church at Corinth were these: 'On the first day of every week, each one of you should set aside a sum of money in keeping with his income, saving it up, so that when I come no collections will have to be made.' (1 Corinthians 16:2)

The question of just how much we should give was well illustrated by a Christian minister whom I once heard exclaim, 'Blow the money, put yourselves on the offertory plate!'

Meditating upon the subject over the years, my approach to tithing has crystallised into the following principles:

Am I, as a servant of the Lord, recognising his claim on all I possess?

Am I a steward of my possessions?

Do I just drop something in the collection plate, or do I plan to give, thoughtfully and intelligently, a regular amount?

> Take my silver and my gold,
> Not a mite would I withhold.

The Master who entrusts us with possessions and

money commands us to use them for his glory, and for the blessing of our fellow men, just as Sopan did.

JUST A THOUGHT: MONEY TALKS—WHAT DOES YOURS SAY?

CHAPTER NINE

Oh Nurse!

MY initiation into nursing must have made many a hospital farce appear somewhat mundane.

During my general nurse training opinions of me varied widely. Although there were the odd one or two tutors who thought I was brilliant, the large majority looked on me as a steady reliable nurse whilst one, whom we nick-named Polly, regarded me of strictly limited ability, not quite right in the head. The situation was due to several unfortunate, mostly harmless, but now unmentionable pranks, typical of the young students' mentality.

For the first twelve weeks of State Registration training, as it was then known, we were sent to a Preliminary Training School in what was once a large Victorian manor, not far from London's Ealing Common.

'Here you will learn, and learn well,' declared Polly, perspiring profusely because of her uncontrolled hyperthyroidism. 'Here you begin to be nurses. I am like a jug full of knowledge, and I shall attempt to pour it into your upper receptacles, otherwise known as your minute brains, tiny little things inside your skulls; all this basic stuff will be absorbed before you lot are let loose on the poor, unsuspecting patients—heaven help 'em !'

One never to be forgotten day, under the watchful eye of beaky Polly, we were truly let loose upon the poor unsuspecting patients. My day was spent on the men's surgical ward.

'Nurse.'

Nothing.

'NURSE!'

Suddenly realising the sister was calling me, I straightened up, smoothed down my spanking new, over-sized uniform and, smiling, bustled my way to where she was waiting.

'When I call you, nurse, you never keep *me* waiting,' she bellowed. 'Do you understand?'

'Yes, sister.'

'Is there something amusing you?'

'No, sister.'

'Well, wipe that silly grin off your face.'

'Yes, sister,' I said, obeying in a less confident tone, lowering my eyes.

'Now listen to me. Mr. Morgan is one of our patients who has been very ill and has to stay on bed rest. He needs the toilet. See to him,' she ordered. 'So, go on then—don't just stand there looking dense.'

I scurried along to a bedside, greeting the grumpy occupant as Mr. Morgan.

'I ain't him, nurse. You want ol' Bert. He's over there in that bed,' he said, indicating Mr. Morgan's bed. That's it, that one.'

Bert Morgan appeared agitated.

'I need the commode, nurse' he said. 'I really can't wait much longer.'

I did not know what to do because sister had stressed the severity of his illness and his needing to remain on bed rest. What was I to do? How could he remain on bed rest and use the commode at the same time? A couple of minutes later I, brain of Britain, had solved the problem. Bert Morgan was perched on a commode which, in turn, I had lifted on to his bed.

When the sister marched along to see how I was coping,

she was aghast to see the head of the terrified Mr. Morgan peering at her above the screens!

Polly on hearing about my day glared at me. 'I'll never forget your name, Nurse Wiseman, not ever. For the whole three years of your training, I shall keep my little beady eye on you,' she stated, mopping the beads of perspiration from her brow.

She kept her word. If I so much as passed she'd stop to stare, as if I were bad smell.

Apart from speaking to my family about my faith a year or so previously, I'd tended to mix only with Christians. When I began hospital work in earnest I immediately joined the Christian Fellowship, once again primarily mixing with believers. I'd never actually mingled with any worldly types, certainly I'd never taken a stand for what I believed.

I found it easier to either take a stand or keep quiet when I was surrounded by other like-minded souls, but when I happened to be the odd one out, well, that was a whole new ball game.

During one shift on the gynaecology ward I was standing outside the sister's office, sandwiched between two of the loudest, worldliest student nurses it was possible to meet. Suddenly I noticed a ladder in one of my stockings (no tights allowed in those days!) 'Damn!' I exclaimed, to show I was one of the girls.

Dr Pentecost (yes, that really was his name) emerged from the sister's office. 'Tell me nurse,' he said to me, pointing to my chest. 'What is that little blue badge you have on your uniform?'

My face flushed pink. 'Um... that's my Nurses' Christian Fellowship badge,' I mumbled, wishing the others weren't there to hear.

'Really?', he queried. 'Then live up to it, for you'll have no right to wear such a badge if you continue to use bad language. Take a stand for the Lord. Witness for him.'

His words shot through me like electricity and I went aside, telling the Lord I was sorry. I asked him to give me the strength to witness for him, to speak only the words he wanted me to speak.

The following afternoon, with a letter to write, I went into the Nurses' Sitting Room. Normally the room was crowded, but that day was different; there was just one other student, a petite, pretty, redheaded lass.

'Hi' , she said. 'Can I ask you something?'

'Sure. What is it?'

'It's well... it's that blue badge on your uniform. What's it for?'

Now I really was on the spot. There was no running away or hiding in the shadows of others this time. 'That's my Nurses' Christian Fellowship badge. I'm a Christian.'

She frowned. 'Aren't we all Christians?' she asked. 'I'm certain I must be because I was baptised a Roman Catholic, which makes me a Christian; so why don't I have a badge, too?'

I shook my head. I'd been taught over the last two years that, although there were Christians in the Roman Catholic Church, Catholicism itself was beyond the pale.

'Being a Christian is to know you are a sinner and to find Christ as your Saviour from that sin,' I began.

'But, Janice, I regularly go to confession and the priest frees me from sin.'

'I'm afraid it's not as simple as that.'

She looked quizzical.

I continued to explain that it was the awful, intolerable burden of our sin, and seeing it laid upon him. 'For,' I said, 'that is what happened when Jesus hung on the cross. During those awful moments, God took the sins of the world and laid it upon him.'

'I think I know that,' she said, thoughtfully. 'I have a crucifix over my bed which reminds me of his death.'

'But it's what the Bible says,' I protested.

'Oh, I don't have a Bible—I just depend on what the priest tells me.'

I ignored her. 'Jesus was made sin for us, yet he knew no sin. Because sin had to be atoned for—well, had he not suffered the penalty, we'd each have to suffer, and the wages of sin is death, eternal misery, hell.'

Her eyes opened wide. 'Gosh, Janice, you do seem to know a lot.'

'Ah!' I wish I did. All I do know is that, in that place of shame, God was in Christ, reconciling us to himself, bearing our punishment. That was his part in our salvation.'

She frowned. 'So then, my baptism and confirmation didn't make me a Christian—'

'If we accept what he offers, if we yield our lives in thanksgiving and obedience, we become his grateful, loving, free disciples.'

Tears came into my friend's eyes. 'I'd like him in my life right now. But how...?

'Why don't we kneel down together?'

'And do what?'

I beamed. 'We'll ask Jesus to come into your life.'

We got down on the floor and, through her great racking sobs, Catherine Smythe-Roberts asked the Lord to be her Saviour.

One of Polly's colleagues was firmly convinced that I did little or no academic work for the whole of my training, and now it was nearing my finals; both the Hospital's and the State's.

'I can't see you passing, Nurse Wiseman,' she said, shaking her head. 'Not unless ol' St. Jude gives you a helping hand.'

It came to my notice that I was entitled to a couple of week's holiday, so just before the exams, laden down by piles of text books, I went along to the Common Cold Centre, then situated not far from Salisbury Plain. When I wasn't succumbing to daily nasal sprays, throat swabs and being a general guinea pig in the interests of global science, I had my running nose in a medical text book, frantically making never to be forgotten notes on nursing procedures.

During my two weeks at the Common Cold Centre I not only acquired some cash, but the mother and father of a cold and, on my return to the hospital, I was admitted to the sick bay. Apart from keeping Kleenex in business, I sat up in my hospital bed cramming for my examinations. My friends accused me of trying to get into the *Guinness Book of Records* as swot of the year.

All too soon the day of the examination dawned. Yes, I could answer the first question, and the second, along with everything else that was required of me. Apart from my sore nose, so red it could well have competed with Rudolph's red-nosed reindeer, I felt great. I looked like the Cheshire cat, a grin from ear to ear. I was sure I'd done well, but I joined my colleagues in saying how awful every question was and what would I do if I'd failed.

The results of the Hospital exams were eventually pinned to the notice board in the school of Nursing. I'd passed with marks entitling me to the Silver Medal. Shortly afterwards, the results of my State finals were delivered by the postman. Gingerly, I tore open the large brown envelope. Yes, I was now a qualified nurse.

'Well, now, good old St. Jude, eh?' chuckled Polly's colleague, emerging from Menopause Mansions, the name we youngsters gave to the Sister's Home.

'Who on earth is St. Jude?' I asked, turning to face her full on.

'Oh, he's the saint for hopeless cases,' she explained. 'I prayed to him for you. So, thanks to St. Jude, eh?'

The Tutor even placed 'Thanks to St. Jude' in the personal column of the *Daily Telegraph*!

It was the day of our prize giving and Princess Alexandra was arriving within two hours to hand out any medals and the impressive Hospital certificates.

The entire morning was spent teaching us to march. Matron had employed an ex-Regimental Sergeant Major from her father's old regiment. This big fellow would hopefully lick us into shape once and for all. Matron had planned for our set to be marched into the Grand Hall and, one by one, to present a white-gloved hand to the Princess. She would then shake our hand and present us with our badges, certificates, and medals for the three prize winners. At this moment we had to place our right foot slightly behind the other and give a brief curtsy.

Lined up outside in beautifully pressed uniforms, starched detachable collars rubbing the sides of our necks almost raw, the ex RSM opened his mouth and boomed out, 'By the right… quick…wait fer it… queek march!

Off we went, completely out of step with arms and legs flaying all over the place, giggling as we went.

'Halt!' he boomed even louder, making us bump into the nurse in front, catching her heels with our heavy black lace-ups. 'Well, I never… well, I never did! Never in all my years in the army 'ave I ever seen such a disgraceful lot as wot I 'ave before my very eyes right now. You terrible lot 'ave got ter see 'er Royal 'ighness in next to no time. Nah then, eyes to the front and…'

Suddenly his eyes caught Sally, a tall, very slim, pretty red head. 'Nah then… what 'ave we 'ere? Oh,… no… no, m'girl. You 'aven't an 'ope of marching like that, not never no 'ow! What's the matter with you?' he shouted. 'Stand up straight, shoulders back.'

Sally shuffled, giggled a bit and stood as tall as she was able.

'No... no... no... Nurse. Put yer shoulders back and stick yer chest art, I say.'

Sally wasn't just slender, but almost as flat chested as it was possible to be.

'My chest is out,' she answered. 'It's as out as it will ever be!'

The RSM actually blushed.

Nursing was for me rarely without incident. Just after I'd qualified I found one of my patients dead. An hour later, when a very raw student and I were laying him out, I asked her, for the sake of a form which needed to be completed, what his religion was.

'Jewish,' she replied, nonchalantly.

'WHAT? OH *NO* !' I exclaimed. 'We'll have to un-lay him and quick.'

I knew that the body must not be touched until a rabbi had prayed over him.

The dead Jew was somehow prised back into his pyjamas and warmed up with blankets.

The rabbi, looking not unlike my late grandfather, commented that the body was a bit stiff. We volunteered nothing, but just stood there looking blank.

After the obligatory prayers, the rabbi came along and told us that the body could be laid out. So 'out' we laid him again.

With the body ready for the mortuary, I called for the porters who couldn't get their trolley up to the ward; the lift was out of order—again.

'Can't you simply carry the body down?' I asked.

'No, Staff. We ain't paid to 'andle no corpse, are we, Sid?'

Sid shook his head. 'Well, Staff, Oi suggest yer git advice from Matron,' advised the fellow. 'Dunt yer fink she should, Sid?'

Sid agreed, stuffing his hands into his pockets and nodding as if his head was on a spring.

Matron suggested the two men pushed their trolley to the back, to the fire escape; the student and I should carry the body down, for it would be unlikely anyone would be in the vicinity to see us. She came along to see her unusual plan put into action.

A third of the way down the semi-spiral fire escape the air came out of the dead Jew's lungs, like a deep sigh. The student, unaware that this sound often happened, screamed and let go. He was much too heavy for me and I dropped him; he landed at Matron's feet with a mighty big thud.

Another occasion involved some Asians—bless 'em. A Pakistani woman died from status asthmaticus. The grief-stricken family requested her body be flown back to Pakistan, but not knowing how to go about it they approached me.

I rang a Registrar for births, marriages and deaths who said they would have to acquire certain documents, along with providing a box (a coffin) for her.

I passed on the message to the next of kin.

'OK,' they replied and promptly went on their way.

About two or three hours later the two men returned carrying a gigantic cardboard box, previously used by the supermarket to store Kellogg's cornflakes. 'Will this do?' they asked.

A PRAYER

O Lord, give me the strength to witness for you and to speak only the words you want me to say.

CHAPTER TEN

Tragic Loss

I WAS the chairperson of a small committee which had the oversight of the local branch of the Inter-Hospitals' Nurses' Christian Fellowship.

I not only enjoyed the IHNCF gatherings, but they were golden opportunities for spiritual growth. We were a mixed bag—Baptists, Anglicans, Brethren, Pentecostals and Methodists; but denominations didn't seem to matter overmuch, for we were bound together by one faith in our Lord, having a genuine love for each other.

One of our regular attenders was a delightful Christian, a pretty lass named Sophie, the only and much loved daughter of a Pentecostal couple; they didn't live too far from her at the Hospital.

After a tiring day's work in casualty, my room-mate, Helen, and I were slowly trudging up the seemingly endless stone staircase to our room on the fourth floor of the Nurses' Home; every stair seemed to get steeper by each step.

Stopping in my tracks, I frowned. 'Can you smell gas?' I asked, as we approached our landing.

Sniffing, she at first shook her head, accusing me of being related to the bloodhound family; then she agreed. 'It seems to be coming from the kitchen,' she said.

A tiny kitchen had been kitted out for the nurses' basic use. Home Sister equipped it with a sink, some pots and pans, crockery and cutlery, along with a second-hand gas cooker. If we couldn't be bothered to traipse down to the main dining room, we could make ourselves something to eat. Each floor had a similar kitchen, and we were all grateful to Home Sister for her thoughtfulness. She appeared to be a hard nut to crack but, deep down, she was as soft as butter.

'Pooh! It's bad, isn't it?' I said, holding the back of my hand under my nostrils.

As the two of us were just about to investigate there was a small explosion, yet loud enough to startle us both. 'Oh, no,' I gasped, squinting to try to make out who it was, what had caused it.

'It's... it's Sophie, isn't it?' Helen spluttered. 'I'm sure it's her.'

Coughing and choking, Helen and I managed to get into the kitchenette and drag Sophie out into the airy corridor. Daisy, a cleaner, pushing her mop, stopped to stare; I instructed her to put out an emergency call.

Helen scowled at the woman. 'Cardiac arrest! It's an emergency. Go on, Daisy, move...' she shouted. 'Go to the internal phone—phone 545.'

Helen attempted to give mouth-to-mouth resuscitation, but it was difficult to maintain a clear airway; the apparent gas explosion had burnt much of Sophie's face. Feeling no pulse, I was pounding on the girl's chest, desperately trying to get her heart working again.

We both knew her burns needed urgent attention, but the two of us were well aware that resuscitation took first priority. There's not much use in treating the burns of a dead person.

Suddenly, in response to the emergency call sent out by Daisy, the cleaner, there were two or three doctors and several experienced nursing staff shoving us out of their way and, as they were treating her, Sophie was being raced along to the Hospital's Intensive Care Unit, the theatre staff on stand-by.

We hurried behind the emergency team but, as we reached the ICU the door was slammed shut in our faces. Sophie, one of our closest friends from the Nurses' Christian Fellowship, was being treated in there and we were prevented from being with her. Helen and I felt helpless, in the way, but out of the way.

Helen, as if half in a daze, dropped down on a solitary upright chair. Already bone tired and almost completely exhausted, now so upset, Helen kept gulping to rid herself of the lump in her throat, looking up to blink away the blinding tears until rivulets ran down her cheeks.

Leaning hard against the cold wall, I slowly slid my way down, sitting with a thud on the tiled floor. A tear rolled down my face, then another. 'What if she dies?' I began. 'What if...'

My room-mate glared at me. 'Shut up' she snapped. 'Just please, Janice, shut up. OK? I can't bear to think of the worst.'

After an hour or so, two equally tired doctors appeared from within the confines of the Intensive Care Unit.

I struggled to my feet. 'Please can you tell us how our friend is?', I questioned. 'Please...'

Helen stood up and pushed in front of me, facing Dr. Dyson, the senior of the two. 'Her name is Sophie Tyler,' she said. 'We were the ones who found her and...'

We stared, urging him to tell us. Waiting, I clenched my fists so hard that my nails almost penetrated the palms of my hands.

Dr. Dyson frowned. 'Well, it seems Sophie took about twenty Seconal, strong sleeping tablets, and then, to make doubly sure, she tried to gas herself.'

'The oven must have had a fault, for somehow it exploded,' I added.

He nodded. 'We're keeping her on a breathing machine, but we really don't hold out much hope,' he said.

'Why on earth she did such an awful thing, well, it's an enigma. Anyway, her parents are on their way here, so perhaps they'll throw some light on the situation. But, the main thing is to get Sophie stabilised...'

With her parents at her side, helpless to do anything but listen to the noisy sounds of the life-support machine, they sat and prayed until everything stopped. Sophie had been diagnosed as brain dead. All hope was gone. At that very moment it was as if the whole world had been switched off and was in total and utter silence. Sophie was dead.

Her parents blamed themselves, for they'd had an argument with Sophie over her boy friend—they had disapproved of the colour of his skin, of all things. Sophie, it seems, was also worried she'd fail her finals, despite the fact she was a brilliant nurse—she just couldn't cope with failure.

The funeral service was held a week or so later at the Pentecostal church where she'd been brought up and where her parents were active members.

In full uniform I, along with many others, entered the church. The large airy building was filling up fast. I moved into a pew on the right hand side of the church. Slowly sitting down, I tried to say a brief prayer, yet my mind seemed a blank. Sitting upright, I stared at the flower covered coffin, realising that Sophie's body was in there. I began to wonder if Helen and I had worked hard enough, in the first place, to resuscitate the girl. Had we failed her? But it was too late for such recriminations. My whole body began to tremble and I wanted to cry, but I did'nt—not then. A Nursing Sister, also a born-again Christian, was sitting in the pew immediately behind mine. She leaned forward and squeezed my left shoulder. Her touch was meant as a comfort, but I couldn't cope—not any longer. I needed to get out. As the first hymn, 'Praise my soul, the King of heaven' was announced I pushed my way past, and climbed over the others on my left and fled out of the building.

After the interment all the joy seemed to disappear from many of us. Sadness overwhelmed me. I was unable to handle the tragedy; unable to understand why God allowed her death. Some Christian nurses reasoned it all away by sermonising about free will, but I didn't know.

The Christian Fellowship meetings ceased and many of the members either moved on to other situations, or slipped back in their Christian way. One nurse was so severely affected by the tragedy that she was sectioned and admitted to the Maudsley Psychiatric Hospital, London

It was a bad time.

I came to the decision it was time I too moved on. In September 1968, I was accepted as a pupil midwife at the British hospital for Mothers and Babies in Woolwich, London.

MEDITATION

Is there a need for renewal, that my life may be used again?

CHAPTER ELEVEN

Called to Serve

"Open your eyes and look at the fields!
They are ripe for harvest."

(John 4:35)

I WAS half-way through my midwifery training, and today had been a happy one; I'd delivered a woman, who'd been trying for years for a baby, of a healthy son. But now it was half-past five and, at this precise moment, I had other concerns. Unexpectedly, I'd been asked by a more mature friend to take her little Sunday School class, for she wasn't feeling too well.

'Honestly, Lynda, I'm really not the person to ask. I know virtually nothing about Sunday School teaching,' I protested, bringing up one excuse after the other. 'In fact, I've never been to a Christian Sunday School.'

She assured me it would be no irksome duty; that on this particular Sunday I would not have to do very much more than just supervise the children, so there wouldn't even be any preparation.

'Someone from the Methodist Missionary Society will be visiting to talk about his work; I'm pretty certain he'll be showing some of his slides. All you'll have to do is to welcome him and keep the children in some sort of order. See, Janice, there'll be nothing to it,' she croaked. 'You will do it for me, won't you? Please say you will. Everyone else seems too busy...'

'So, you mean I'm your last resort?' I grinned. 'Just as well I have the weekend off.'

It was nothing like as easy as Lynda had made out. After opening in prayer, singing a few choruses with the 'little darlings' whilst attempting to play an out of tune 'honky-tonk' type of piano before introducing the speaker, I had one of those terrible moments when one's mind goes blank—I forgot his name! Yet I think maybe I half got away with it by saying, 'This afternoon, children, we have an overseas worker who's going to tell us a little about his work, and show us some of his slides. Now, I'll leave him to introduce himself...'

All the children clapped, cheered and whistled—the sort of whistle that is produced when they put two fingers in their mouths and the sound that comes out is a terrible piercing noise.

One of the missionary's final slides vividly illustrated a large golden cornfield, gently waving in the wind with the crop ready for harvesting. 'Perhaps, one day, God might call one of you to be a harvester for him', he said. 'There will be many souls lost to God if there is no-one to tell them about his salvation.'

I do not know if God spoke to any of the children in that meeting, but I realised, for the first time in my life, that there was a sphere of service to which I was being called; I was now prepared to go wherever he wanted me.

Some weeks later four young Christian friends from Westminster Chapel told me they were going to Herne Bay Court for a weekend conference, run by the Poona and Indian Village Mission operating in Western India; they invited me to go along, too.

It was, for me, a memorable weekend when I learned of that great continent and I began to develop a compassion for those without Christ. Was God calling me to be a harvester in India? If so, I needed to keep that goal in view and never to put it on hold.

Through the reading of Colossians 1:11 the Lord began to show me my need of patience. Patience! A quality my closest relatives and friends rarely saw in me, for I either wanted something or other performed right then or 'yesterday'.

So it was that the following two and a half years were, to me, an irksome test! Many of God's choice servants have had to learn the hard lessons of patience. For example, David was anointed to be King of Israel, but had to wait many years, until the death of Saul, before he became king. During this time of waiting, many trials and tribulations came his way, but out of them all David was able to say, 'I waited patiently for the Lord' (Psalm 40:1). Now God was about to teach me the hard lesson of moving in *his* time instead of advancing within my own schedule.

I was so keen to go overseas that, in my naivety, any place would do, just as long as I was a missionary! (My impatience could have led me down a wrong path.)

I started attending a prayer meeting for the Red Sea Mission Team. This was held in the Finchley home of Dr and Mrs Gurney, and it was there that I occasionally met missionaries on furlough. It occurred to me that God might want me as one of their missionary recruits; but someone, in their wisdom, pointed out to me the danger of a Jewess working in a Moslem culture.

Then there was the valedictory service, held at Westminster Chapel, for one of the members who was leaving to work overseas with the Grenfell Mission. I quickly abandoned any thoughts of working in the frozen waste lands. It was not for me!

Realising that I wasn't going to be of use to any missionary society whilst entertaining so many crazy romantic notions, I decided to spend as much time as I could, apart from my own quiet time, praying each day, seeking the *Lord's* will for my life.

It was then, at about the age of twenty-two, with my nursing and midwifery qualifications under my belt, that I responded in a positive way to his call by applying to Mount Hermon Missionary Training College, situated in one of the fairly pleasant suburbs of West London.

Having been accepted as a student, I naively considered that, in the almost perfect setting of such a college, it would be much easier to live a holy and more dedicated life; yet it didn't quite work out like that. I brought myself with me, and all the other students turned up with themselves, too.

One of my room mates, Rachel, voiced the high opinion that any sense of fun, especially mine, was beneath her. She was just too good to be true! Totally incompatible, it was most difficult to live together, despite all my efforts.

Sarah, our other room-mate, was a loud, giggly lass who knitted a lot. When those needles started clacking I half wanted to strangle her! I was nearer to my crime when she used either the wash-basin or the bath. She simply pulled the plug, leaving it for either Rachel or me to clean. Even more unpleasant was her way of icing the bathroom floor with a layer of talc.

To crown it all, if a student became irritated by certain matters in the Bible College, the phrase Good Missionary Training or GMT tripped from the lips of the others. It was generally said in a jolly fashion when one was called upon to do something particularly horrid, such as eating luke-warm porridge topped with prunes. It was said so often to me that I felt, at times, my chances of becoming a good missionary were slim.

It is probably never easy for those in their mid-twenties, who have already earned their place as adults in a secular sphere, to come again under authority in such a college.

During my first week at college the bursar required payment of fees. I lingered at the back of the line. Emma, who stood directly in front of me, took out a cheque book from her handbag and, turning to me, asked if I had a pen she could borrow.

'Yes, sure, a pen is about all I do have,' I smiled thinly.

She looked quizzical.

I explained I'd been praying the Lord would provide my fees. 'Now here I am, almost as poor as a church mouse,' I whispered. 'I do believe that I am meant to be here, but...'

'Well, then, if you are meant to be here, I'm sure God will provide your fees,' interrupted Emma.

'What? Before I get to the front of this queue?' I asked with a grin.

Finally, all the students had paid their term fees. Only I alone was left.

'Er, my name is Janice Wiseman, I firmly believe God has called me to this particular college and I have prayed he would provide my fees. However...'

'Please, do stop talking, Janice, and I'll explain,' she smiled. 'Your fees for the whole two years have already been sorted out. I also have an allowance to hand over to you so your personal needs will be met. Theological books are very expensive and a cheque for purchasing all the necessary literature is waiting for you in my office. In fact, any expenses you might incur during your time here have been taken care of.'

My eyes widened and I took a step back. 'But... who has given all this money? I asked. 'I come from a wealthy family but they've disowned me, so it's not them.'

'Sorry dear, I'm not at liberty to say. The Christian in question wishes to remain anonymous, so I've been sworn to secrecy.'

I never discovered who paid my college expenses, but

I thanked God for them. Our heavenly Father is faithful—he knew my needs and he provides, through the generosity of one of his obedient servants.

MEDITATION

And my God will meet all your needs according to his glorious riches in Christ Jesus. (Philippians 4:19)

PRAYER

Help me, Lord, to trust you in every part of my life—not just concerning my money, but in my relationships with others, those I like and those I don't. Forgive me when I fail you.

In Jesus' name. Amen.

CHAPTER TWELVE

The Broken Relationship

I WAS late, and in a hurry to finish my bits of shopping. Grabbing my bags, I made for the exit too intent to notice the man heading in the same direction.

There was a moment when either of us could have held back, but although we glanced briefly at each other, neither of us stopped. I thought I was nearer and would get there first; but he moved faster.

We collided in the department store's revolving door, which promptly jammed—with us crushed together in one section. I looked up, my eyes dark, cold, irritated. The eyes that met mine were icy blue.

'If you back out, that will free the door' said his deep voice.

'If you had had the good manners to let me go first this wouldn't have happened. You step back,' I snapped.

It was all his fault, and I didn't like his peremptory tone, or the fact that I had been forced so close to him. You couldn't have got a sheet of paper between us.

He was tall, almost six feet with a face that could have been carved out of granite. He wore casual dress, a thick crew neck jumper and worn jeans, not a bit smart.

'There's no point in arguing about whose fault it is,' he spat out. 'Just wriggle backwards.'

'Any wriggling can be done by you,' I informed him. 'Look, even an idiot should see that the easiest way of freeing the door would be for you to back out,' he pointed out.

'Oh, very well,' I said, shifting sideways to get into a better position for wriggling out, aware we were attracting a crowd.

There were people on the inside of the store, trying to get out, and another couple on the pavement trying to get in, watching us and grinning. We were providing live entertainment and I felt very silly. He finally squeezed backwards, and I immediately pushed the revolving door, murmuring an apology to people waiting.

The first day of the beach mission I stood there transfixed with my mouth open. It would be him, wouldn't it?

Of all the men in the world… it had to be that man I got stuck with in the revolving door. He was smiling, gesturing.

'I'm Bill,' he said. 'A theological student.'

Numbly, I held out my hand. He said something polite and distant. I answered with equal remoteness. He released my hand and I had a sort of sinking feeling. I explained that I too was at a Missionary Training College.

On the last day of the mission, Bill beamed in my direction. 'How are you getting back to London,' he asked

'Don't worry about it,' I began. 'There's a regular train service.'

'I have my car. May I drop you off?'

I nodded. 'Thanks,' I said.

His tanned hands gripped the wheel; he turned and gave me a long, cool look. 'I'm glad we've met.'

For the first time I felt myself smiling at him.

The car spun round the corner and began moving along the London streets until it came outside my college.

'Stop here, please.'

He braked and turned toward me, but I was already getting out of the car. I slammed the door, then bent towards the window. He leaned over to wind it down.

I looked into his gleaming eyes. 'I'll phone you,' he said.

Back in college, I confided in my friend, Jilly, concerning Bill.

'Maybe your chemistry will really mix...' she giggled. 'You know, when you meet again.'

'Chemistry?' I interrupted. 'Rot. In my experience it has always made nitro-glycerine.'

'Well, you are going to see each other again?'

'Probably. He said he'd 'phone me.'

'Well, don't go ahead without permission.'

'What do you mean?' I asked, following her into the bathroom. 'I'm my own person—I can do as I please.'

I sat on the edge of the empty bath while she filled the wash-hand basin, ready to wash her hair. She shoved me aside to reach for her towel, reminding me that I would need the Principal's permission to even sit next to Bill in church, let alone go out with him on a date.

'All these petty, stupid rules. We're not children.'

'GMT', chuckled my companion from underneath her towel.

The Principal did give me permission. Bill and I went to Westminster Chapel. Various dates followed and gradually we became quite fond of each other.

One Saturday afternoon he telephoned me at the college. Another student answered the telephone and called for me.

'Janice, it's the man himself,' she grinned, holding out the telephone receiver.

He'd phoned to ask if he could call for me.

Bill and I set out for the rest of the day in the countryside. Reaching our destination, we just sat for quite a while, silently staring out across the panoramic view. The sun was making an effort to come out, but really not succeeding very well. We got out of the car and Bill put his arm around my shoulders. 'Cold?' he queried.

'No, not really.' 'Happy?' I nodded.

'Janice, I want to ask you something—just to reassure myself.'

He seemed enigmatic. 'What is it?' I enquired.

'It is true for you, isn't it? This overwhelming feeling—it is as true for you as it is for me, isn't it?' he asked, speaking softly.

'Yes, I think so,' I breathed. 'Although we've only known each other for a short while. No. I know so—I know, Bill, that I do love you.'

We must have stayed together for quite a time, walking, holding hands, and enjoying each other's company, laughing and embracing.

When we returned it was getting dark. I remember feeling as though we were on the edge of a precipice. It was then that Bill said how desperately he loved me. He told me that his life would be as nothing without me.

'I really must be going into college. I shall be late,' my voice quaked, nervously.

'Just a little while longer,' he pleaded. 'Don't go in yet.'

I stood my ground, but he told me he'd loved me from the first moment we'd met, and that he would love me until the end of his days. 'When can I see you again?' he asked, a sense of urgency in his voice. 'Next Saturday?'

'No. I'm sorry. I mustn't neglect my studies.'

'Promise me something,' he continued.

'What is it?'

'That you'll meet me next Saturday,' he said. 'Please...'

I began to weaken in my resolve, annoyed with myself.

'I'll pick you up at two o'clock sharp. OK?'

'All right,' I said. 'But not before. I must study.'

'It is just that I'll have something for you, something very special.'

I met him as promised. He kissed me several times. Reaching into his jacket pocket, he brought out a small box.

Opening it, I gasped. 'Oh, it's beautiful!'

He slipped the engagement ring onto the third finger of my left hand. 'Marry me?' he whispered. 'Marry me, my darling.'

Back in college I flashed my solitaire under the noses of my friends, before making my way to the Principal's study where she gave me her blessing. I was so happy, I might as well have been in a seventh heaven.

Wedding plans were put into action. We were to be married at the end of my final term.

One Saturday afternoon Jessica, a friend from Chapel, came with me to choose my wedding gown.

We went to the bridal department of Dickens and Jones in London's Regent Street. There I tried on one dress after another. One in particular caught my eye; it was absolutely beautiful and fitted me like a glove. The sales assistant asked when the wedding was to be.

'Oh, when I've finished college,' I replied, casually.

'She's going to be a minister's wife,' said my friend.

A minister's wife?

'I think I'll leave the dress for now,' I said, unzipping the gown. Jessica and I made our way for a cup of coffee and a slice of gateau.

'What was that display all about?' she enquired, leaning forward.

'Right now I am just so confused, Jess.'

'Bill, what is God calling you to do once you've finished at college?' I asked. 'We really need to discuss our future.'

'Why do you ask? Janice, you know I'm going to be a Baptist minister. You will be my wife.'

Feeling my heart beating, I stiffened up and looked away.

'Janice, what's the matter?' he asked, attempting to hug me close to his chest.

I tugged away. 'Bill, I'm sorry, but I cannot be your wife,' I began, trying to fight back the welling tears. 'God is, you say, apparently calling you to the Baptist ministry here in England, yet he is calling me to India. If I married you… if I stayed in England I'd be out of the Lord's will. Oh, Bill… Bill, it's just been a whirlwind romance. We're not meant for each other.'

We drove back in complete silence. That day was our last day together. The very last day together in all our lives.

As for Bill, the last I heard he was a Baptist minister in South London, married with a couple of children—a boy and a girl.

MEDITATION

Am I waiting for more guidance when the instructions have already been given?

> His hands and feet and heart, all three,
> Were pierced for me on Calvary,
> And here and now, to Him I bring
> My hands, feet, heart, an offering.

CHAPTER THIRTEEN

Six Aussies and One Sheila

MOST overseas missionaries or missionary recruits usually either sail or fly to their chosen destination. However, I heard about Beryl, another medical missionary who, presumably to save on expenses, travelled overland from England to India. With that nurse's adventure buzzing around in my mind, I spoke to the Committee members of the faith mission who'd accepted me, and requested their permission for me to do the same. Surprisingly, they all agreed.

At the time of writing, such an overland trip would be too difficult to contemplate; many of the countries are now either closed to Westerners or are dangerous territories, but, in the sixties and early seventies there was little unrest and such trips were often made, especially by the hippie community.

Six men, three from the Australian outback, two from Perth and one from Brisbane, who had fulfilled their ambitions to see most of Europe, especially all the tourist sights in the United Kingdom, were planning to return home overland starting from York, with room for one more. Seeing their advertisement in the personal column of the *Daily Telegraph*, I applied. Signing my letter just J. Wiseman, I did not even so much as hint I was a woman, for I believed I might be turned down flat. Imagine their intense surprise, shock and horror when we actually came face to face in a place named Stillington, near York.

When I walked into their digs they laughingly shook their heads, telling me how it would be impossible for them to accept me; one young female with six virile fellows could well prove a problem.

'Please, please let me come with you. You see, I need to get across to India,' I explained. 'I'm a qualified nurse and midwife, and I'm going to Bombay to do missionary work.'

'A missionary, eh? Heck, I have never come across a real live missionary before,' chuckled the main spokesman, trying not to explode with actual laughter.

'Well, I dunno. I've never liked holy Joes,' interjected another. 'Anyway, we'd be sleeping mostly in either some pretty grotty hotels, or rough under canvas.'

'Please,' I begged. 'I won't be a moment's trouble.'

'But we might be,' winked another.

'What do ya' think fellas? Shall we give her a chance? After all, a nurse just might prove useful to us,' stated the original spokesman, turning to look at each man in turn for their reactions.

'She can mop my fevered brow anytime,' smiled one man. 'Although I doubt if I'll need her as a midwife.'

I raised my eyes heavenwards, unused to such masculine, jocular behaviour and, seeing I wasn't prepared to tolerate anything near the mark, they began to take me seriously. Realising my urgent desire to get to India, they decided to give me a chance, promising to be honourable and respect my privacy.

Having been accepted, I decided it was best to find out the problems before they found me. Travelling through so many countries, one after the other, raises all sorts of questions, not least the financial. I was no longer in British employment as such—I was owned by the Mission and really living by faith.

I went along to a bank in the West End of London and spoke with the manager, a smart man approaching middle age and dressed in a pin-striped suit.

'Iraq and Iran insist I have a minimum of one hundred pounds all the time I travel through their country,' I explained.

I watched his facial expression, for a hundred pounds in the sixties and seventies was probably twice as much as his monthly take-home pay. He agreed to allow me half the sum in my account. The remainder was to be a love gift from him. It came to light that he himself was a Christian, a regular attender at All Souls, Langham Place.

'Just thinking of awful emergencies...What if I need the hundred pounds?' I asked. 'How easy is it for you to get the money out to me?'

He gave me a code so that he could properly identify me.

Much impressed by the Christian bank manager, I was beginning to feel a touch intrepid as I contemplated the journey that lay before me. However, I hadn't felt fearless and brave at the surgery where I received an armful of injections to prevent tetanus, yellow fever, cholera and typhoid. With a very sore arm and a bottle of malaria tablets rattling in my handbag, I decided to get some fresh air in my lungs.

Strolling through Hyde Park, I bumped into a portly old Jew. Mr Abrahams used to own a small jewellers in Wimbledon. I was slightly apprehensive as to how he would greet me, for he must have heard, through the grapevine, that I'd been ostracised by my Jewish family. I was amazed to find him most friendly.

'How do you cope when something very unusual happens to you?' I queried, sitting beside him on a park bench.'

'Oi become tremendously Briteesh. Oi always speak

Engleesh. It vorks loik a dream. Ven people know you are Briteesh den day respect yoi,' he said in a slow Yiddish accent. 'Oi'm not stupid, for oi 'ave 'eard all about India, yoi know.'

Felix Abraham stopped talking only to throw some bread to the ever-hungry birds and ducks.

'So, yoi are going abroad, eh? Vell, each to 'is own. Dat's vot oi always say. Each to 'is own. Oi know yoi, though. Always 'ave been a determined, independent girl. Vell, Oi think Oi' ll put 2-I on you vill succeed. Oi do not dink, m'dear, dat yoi vould go in for someding and not succeed.'

A bet on a future missionary? It was time to bring the conversation to a close and remember that God called me to serve him as a missionary—not as a racehorse running at 2—1 on.

The day came for the six Australian men to leave from York. On their way down to Folkestone they made a brief stop in Croydon, near the station where they picked up their Sheila—me.

One or two of the men were still cautious concerning this young, female companion. They didn't think I'd last the trip, for it was to be no picnic. The coach arrived at the Ferry Terminal and we disembarked each of us making sure that our luggage was safe.

I had a memorable send-off by many of my Christian friends from Westminster Chapel, others from my nursing days, but most came from Bible College.

They were all singing a hymn as they joined me. A Baptist minister friend gripped both my hands and prayed over me. Each in turn hugged or kissed me on both sides of my face. I choked back the welling tears wondering if I would ever see them on this earth again.

Finally all the Christians sang:

God be with you till we meet again,
May He through the days direct you;
May He in life's storms protect you;
God be with you till we meet again.

God be with you till we meet again;
And when doubts and fears oppress you;
May His holy peace possess you;
God be with you till we meet again.

God be with you till we meet again;
In distress His grace sustain you;
In success from pride restrain you;
God be with you till we meet again.

God be with you till we meet again;
Nay He go through life beside you;
And through death in safety guide you;
God be with you till we meet again.

(Donald Hughes, 1911-1967,
based on J.E.Rankin 1828-1904)

They sang it over again until the Channel ferry departed and their singing faded away into the distance, unable to be heard by me any longer. Finding the whole experience unbearably emotional, I kept swallowing to rid myself of the lump in my throat.

The Australians, at this point, decided they'd all made one of the biggest mistakes of their lives—how, they wondered, would they cope with a holy Joe in tow and for a minimum of three long months; all that singing, praying and Bible study!

The gulls screeched overhead. I took a last lingering

look at Folkestone in the autumn sun. Would it be like this when I got back? Supposing I never returned. I sensed a tightening of my stomach as they cast off the last rope that joined us to the dockside.

MEDITATION

Do I merely argue with non-Christians, or can I challenge their thinking in a thought-provoking way in order to point them to Christ?

CHAPTER FOURTEEN

The Overland Trek

(1971)

WHAT I had taken on was irrevocable; there could be no turning back. I had to go on. The time for talking was past, my face was set steadfastly towards India.

The ferry was almost empty—that was how much air travel was changing things. Yet I found a sense of ease and relaxation about being at sea.

After the Channel crossing, we boarded a train, which was to take us as far as Austria with its crisp mountain scenery. During the train journey I felt as if I should be studying the Indian language or checking timetables, but it was too late for any of that. I found my berth on the train and was soon fast asleep as it duly sped on through the night. The steward woke me next morning with a continental breakfast, informing me that it was a beautiful day outside.

'Where are we?' I enquired, rubbing my eyes.

'Why—the Alps, of course.'

Most important of all, we were heading east all the time and I felt as if I had finally flushed Britain from my system.

We had clocked up the countries on the train with encouraging regularity—Switzerland, Liechtenstein and Austria.

We decided to spend a few days in Austria before boarding another train. In Vienna we had a wonderful meal—what exactly I cannot remember, but we treated ourselves to the works—a grand Euro blow-out! Farewell to the familiar! Not only the food and the culture, but the scenery and life itself would be very different. The leisurely crossing of Europe was a gentle introduction to all that was ahead. We were about to enter a world where things no longer happened the way they did at home in England.

The train arrived in Istanbul and we disembarked. Here we found our way to a garage in the centre of the city where we collected two extra large and apparently purpose-built Land Rovers. Before paying the owner of the garage, Steve, our vehicle expert, insisted that we were allowed a test drive. Everything seemed satisfactory and the long journey eastwards began. At the beginning, we all took turns to drive and, in this way, made good progress. When Steve and Roger drove the rest of us wondered if the vehicles had been modified so that the brakes and the accelerator were directly attached to the horn—very noisy!

Eventually, the driving became too tough for me, so I took on other chores, such as the washing and cooking. The driving was left to the stronger and more experienced men who were used to the rough terrain of the Australian outback.

Weariness was already setting in, which worried me for I had months of travel ahead. I did not want the men to see I was flagging and that it was all becoming too much for me, after all. Pride, I suppose!

Iraq was then a very interesting place. I was fascinated by the people and the way in which they lived. Faces showed energy, curiosity, pride and abundant good humour. One was tempted to shed some English inhibitions and become a part of Baghdad. It was then a wonderful place to watch life; technology co-existed with the old customs. A man with a fez on his head might walk by dressed in Levi denim jeans and trainers, a spectrum of East and West. It was all so different from the Europe we had just left.

The call to prayer coming from the minaret of a nearby mosque rang across the city reminding us that these people were governed by 'the will of Allah'.

Parking our two vehicles, we began to look for a hotel. The first man we stopped was an Iraqi who spoke English, after a fashion. We resisted his invitation to show us the sights and finally persuaded him to direct us to an hotel. Getting to the hotel was not easy and I nearly walked into the traffic head on. The streets were like the Grand Prix circuit!

'You're not in London now, Sport. The traffic doesn't drive on the left here, you know!' teased one of the men.

We turned a corner and found ourselves a rambling hotel that looked as if it had acne. Nevertheless, the lure of a comfortable bed and a bath was great. I had not been able to have a proper bath since leaving London.

'Have you enough bedrooms for us all?' asked Mike.

'We have eight million bedrooms', replied the hotelier.

After our laughter died down I was installed in a single room on the second floor. At the end of a long, hot, tiring day I was just longing to soak in a hot bath. I turned on the taps. At first there was a loud banging noise in the pipes and then discoloured water came out in short bursts. Some bath! Anyway, I had a bed.

This hotel, had it been in London, would have been closed down by the 'powers that be'. But here, in Baghdad, it was of an acceptable standard!

We decided the next morning that hotels were not going to be the 'norm'. It took too long to find suitable places. Camping out under the stars, or in the back of the Land Rover was cheaper, cleaner and safer for me; after all, women in Muslim countries usually do not go around unveiled and on their own. I was breaking all the rules!

We would need to take provisions with us from now on. But what? It would be hot and there would be no means of refrigeration.

Ah, well, start simple, I thought.

'I need to buy some rice. We are going on a long journey, so I need rice for seven people,' I said to the market trader, who thankfully spoke a little English.

'I have ten kilogramme sacks of best rice,' he said.

'I hope you like rice!' I smiled, turning to the six men who were waiting behind me to carry the sacks, the crates of mineral water, toilet rolls, tins of meat and everything else Western travellers seem to need. Life was introducing me to many new experiences and, working as a team to ensure our survival, was also 'good missionary training' for me.

We needed to make ourselves comfortable. As a protection from the heat a tarpaulin was placed over our sacks of provisions which made up the new floors of the Land Rovers. Great for sleeping on!

This nomadic life would, I felt, take some getting used to. I needed to remember, for instance, that the sun went down very quickly and, once it was gone, there were no electric lights. So, immediately after tea, we got our bedding sorted out. We had to pump up seven camping mattresses with foot pumps. It was not too bad as long as we did not get a puncture! I bought my mattress and bedding in Istanbul about two hours before we left the city. They did not seem to have many camping shops and I had great difficulty getting kitted out before it was time to pack up and go.

The men laughed at my beautifully embroidered pillowcase and I put up with quite a lot of good-natured banter.

'Oh, yes, very nice. Goes with my pretty blue eyes, don't you think?', joked Joe, smoothing down his eyebrows!

I bought extra blankets, but it was so hot at night that we did not need them. In a temperature of 90 degrees Fahrenheit we slept under the stars without additional covering.

One day, when travelling, one of the Land Rovers came to a stop. Steam was billowing out of the engine—all to do with the water cooling system. After what seemed an eternity, the men sorted out the problem whilst I brewed tea for everyone. Knowing I was going to India, the men often called me their 'char wallah'!

A new pattern of life began. Up at first light and a visit to the loo. The lavatory was very basic; we favoured the 'hole in the ground behind a bush' system. Using it was nowhere near as alarming as getting to it—scorchingly hot by day and suicidal at night. Nevertheless, one enjoyed direct contact with nature but it gave 'Miss Prim and proper', as the men called me, rather a shock for I felt very embarrassed with men in the vicinity. However, we were to be together for months and I could not wait that long!

Breakfast was always over by 7.30 a.m. and I had to think about washing the rice for lunch before we moved off. I concocted three meals for seven of us every day. The food was simple but nourishing and no one complained; at least they did not complain to me!

I was pleased with my culinary successes, especially when I recalled some of the disasters that happened in my kitchen in London!

We did not have many incidents of food poisoning and the kind of stomach upsets associated with the East. We were as hygienic as it was possible to be under the circumstances, but I do remember one beautiful, clear, starlit night when I was taken ill with 'Delhi belly' and needed to make several trips to the 'pulpit', the name given to the lavatory by the Australians! At least I had the stars to guide me to the appointed place, but the next morning I was very tired. For a while after this, just the thought of making the men their meals made me want to go home. I felt that if I stayed still and no one mentioned food then I would be all right, but the men were unsympathetic and kept asking if I was looking forward to a nice Bombay Curry!

I longed for a cool, comfortable room with a bath and a decent bed—a place to be still and alone; but this was not to be and I needed to make a recovery without them.

Every day our main meal was over by 5.30 p.m. and there was nothing else to do but to prepare for bed again. The only evening entertainment was provided by me as I washed and undressed under a long loose robe that covered me completely from the neck down—it was held in place by a draw string round my neck. The men, who displayed little modesty, laughed at the wriggling that went on under the 'thing'—they laughed so much that their sides ached and tears ran down their sunburnt faces. By eight o'clock I was usually asleep on the sacks in the Land Rover whilst the men camped outside. I felt safe, unrushed and relaxed.

We made progress slowly. The heat and bad road conditions slowed us down to only 100 miles every twenty-four hours and we had to get used to not hurrying.

Crossing over the frontier to Iran we remembered that this land, which was once called Persia, had a long history going back to the Persian Empire of over 2000 years ago. It was a land of stark contrasts. Crude oil production is the main base of the economy and the country earns great revenue from it. Yet we saw extreme poverty here which we did not see anywhere else. Most of the population is rural and *very* poor.

My encounter with the poor made me wish that I possessed a quick remedy for abolishing poverty. We gave some nourishing rusk-type biscuits to an Iranian family that were desperately hungry and obviously suffering from gross malnutrition.

'I wish we had so much more to give them, Joe,' I said, with a feeling of inadequacy.

'If IRAN ruled the world—' he sang at the top of his voice with a play on the words.

'Do you always have to pretend to be so tough and void of any human emotion?' I asked him, crossly, giving his chest a push.

He just gave me a big grin. However, later, I realised just how much I had misjudged the fellow when I discovered him hugging some very hungry children to whom he was giving candy bars and rusks.

During our travels in Iran we decided to savour the experiences of everyday life there.

'Welcome to our country,' said the camel monger.

We were told by him that we would enjoy the camel ride and he promised to take a photograph of us all having *fun*!

'Lean back as the camel stands up and hold on tight,' the camel monger instructed.

'Oo-oh! Ah-h! I don't like it! *Get me off!*' I yelled when my stomach seemed to come up to my throat as the lumbering creature got to its feet, casting a superior glance at the mortal for whom he toiled. No one took any notice of my cries and so, looking like seven 'Lawrences of Arabia', we set off gingerly on the growling beasts. I suddenly knew why they were called '*ships* of the desert'—they made me feel seasick!

We were aware that the most difficult and dangerous part of our journey was ahead and that it would be an advantage to travel as light as possible. We were carrying too much luggage and a lot of it was mine! Women are apparently notorious for overpacking and I was no exception. So, whilst in Iran, I sent my entire large luggage, mostly books, on to India. That left space enough for the seven of us, our bare necessities and basic provisions.

Our plan was that some should sleep in the Land Rovers whilst others took it in turns to drive, thereby keeping us going both day and night when passing through the danger zones of Afghanistan.

Having crossed the border into Afghanistan, we were warned about the bandits that operated in the mountainous areas there. We were both emotionally tense and physically cold during this stretch of the journey. We came from the intense heat of Iraq and Iran straight into the Afghan winter. I cannot remember another time when I have been so cold—it was freezing!

We all slept in fur hats, thick anoraks, woollen gloves, warm trousers and leather boots. We huddled together for extra warmth. It was so cold that we did not dare take off any clothing, not even to wash!

We felt relatively safe in Kabul and other large cities and towns, but elsewhere it was a very different story and extreme caution had to be observed at all times. The tribesmen in the rugged mountainous areas were nearly always armed and we knew that bandits sometimes attacked travellers passing through. We possessed no weapons to protect ourselves so we just kept going—the men still taking it in turns to drive or navigate.

I must admit to being very scared in Afghanistan. Being so frightened made me feel a bit guilty. Was I not able to trust the Lord, who said, 'Fear not'? I kept reading the words from Joshua, chapter 1, verse 9: 'Have I not commanded you? Be strong and of good courage; be not frightened, neither be dismayed; for the Lord your God is with you, wherever you go.' (RSV) I was the only Christian in the group and *I* was the fearful one. However, the six men did not see me as a poor witness but just as a woman who was not expected to be very tough.

Having passed safely through Afghanistan and then the Khyber Pass, we eventually arrived in Nepal—a Hindu kingdom situated in the magnificent Himalayas. It was here we realised our supplies of European food were running out and we were all feeling very hungry. Throughout the journey we were very careful what kinds of food we ate. Everything was boiled carefully for a minimum of three minutes. Clean water was preserved like gold dust. We never ate a salad because we did not know how it was grown or indeed how it was prepared. No one wanted to eat salad washed in contaminated water! Here in Nepal everything looked very unhygienic and dirty. Nevertheless, we agreed to chance the food because we all desperately needed something to eat.

'Make sure you cook 'em well. Okay?' Ben swore at the waiter as he shouted for seven big buffalo steaks. He then looked at me, sighed and apologised for using bad language. I used to get fed up with the six men always apologising to me for their language.

'Reform would be more acceptable,' I muttered under my breath.

We ate well and were apparently none the worse for eating the buffalo steaks. As we tucked into the food we talked over our adventures. Europe seemed an age away and we could hardly believe all that had happened. Whilst we talked I noticed that Tony seemed unusually quiet and almost sleepy.

'Tony, are you OK?' I asked, giving his shoulder a gentle shake.

Tony was becoming drowsier by the minute.

'What has he eaten that we haven't?', I quizzed the other men.

Four of them shrugged and shook their heads.

However, Roger remembered seeing Tony sampling some of the local honey. That surely must be harmless enough. Tony was more than drowsy—he was slipping into unconsciousness.

One of the students from Bible College, who was two years ahead of me there, had married a medical missionary and they were working together in Kathmandu. I planned to look them up during my brief stay in the country.

'Do you know where your friend's husband hangs out?' asked one of the men.

'I have an address, but I do not know how to find it. Kathmandu is a big place,' I replied, as I flipped over the pages of my small address book.

'Hurry up, will you, with that address? Tony isn't getting better, you know,' Joe snapped.

We enquired from some locals as to the whereabouts of Dr. and Mrs. Michaels and finally discovered that their home was on the outskirts of the city. After a few wrong turns we finally arrived at the Michaels' home.

'Janice! Oh, how wonderful to see you here. Bless you! When did you arrive? Oh, come in, come in!', exclaimed Pamela Michaels, giving me a hug.

'My friend Tony is sick, Pam, and we need help. Is your husband in?' I asked her, great urgency in my voice.

'Yes, bring your friend in,' she replied, calling to her husband to come.

Three men carried Tony into the house and placed him on a couch in Jeremy Michaels' tiny consulting room.

'Mmm. Yes, it's the honey. That's what's causing his unconscious state, right enough. I've seen it quite a few times before,' declared Jeremy.

The contents of Tony's stomach had already been absorbed and so a 'wash-out' was useless. A drip was put in his arm and his airway was kept clear at all times. After twenty-four hours of care Tony showed good signs of recovery and we all fussed around our beloved companion and friend as if he was Lazarus returning from the dead!

Apparently, some honey in Nepal can be lethal. The bees collect the pollen from the poisonous rhododendrons that grow in profusion there and the honey, which they make, causes severe sickness, as Tony found to his cost.

After a few days Tony improved and it was time to say our good-byes to Jeremy and Pamela Michaels. Whilst the men went ahead to explore the night life of Kathmandu I stayed back for just a few hours with Pam and Jeremy who laid hands on me and prayed over me. I felt spiritually refreshed after fellowship with them.

My Australian companions and I were together for just over three months. No one in particular seemed to be the leader for each person in the team had a part to play. I remember Joe more than the others because of the way he teased and tormented me over my Christian commitment.

I remember vividly the occasion when Joe found a scorpion in the desert. He saw I was terrified so he surrounded it with a ring of petrol and set fire to it. Realising that there was no way out, the scorpion brought up its tail and stung itself to death.

'Hey, Janice, that scorpion is a bit like the poor heathen being surrounded by missionaries—no way out!' he teased.

I flashed my dark brown eyes at him.

It was time for me to part from the men and I felt sad to leave the group. I'd trusted my life to the six men and they responded with unquestioning generosity and openness. I knew I should never again enjoy such simple and straightforward friendships as I made with the six men. The names of Joe, Ben, Tony, Roger, Mike and Steve will always remain in my memory. I sometimes wonder what has happened to them and whether they are now married with children of their own. At the moment of separation it was almost impossible to think that I should never see them again. They were nice people. They hugged me and said their good-byes.

I suddenly felt so very alone as I boarded the aeroplane to India and waved good-bye to my friends for the last time. I felt as if I were going to the Siberian Salt Mines as a punishment instead of to the place God had chosen for me. I felt panicky and wanted to run anywhere as long as it was far away from my future sphere of service.

MEDITATION

John Bunyan portrayed the Christian life as being like a journey. Am I any further on today in my spiritual pilgrimage than I was yesterday?

CHAPTER FIFTEEN

Gateway to India

'A great door for effective work has opened to me.'
(1 Corinthians 16:9)

A KALEIDOSCOPE of colour and vivid images awaits the traveller to India, a complex country with the ability to steal the heart of any tourist. As a missionary I doubted whether I would ever have the time to see many of the sights of India. The time that I now possessed was my only chance. I decided to send a wire to Claire Decker at the mission station and ask her to postpone meeting me at Bombay Station for a further week or so. I planned to see the famous golden triangle of Delhi, Agra and Jaipur. A week crammed with sights and sounds which still remain in my memory, an introduction to a land far too complex to even begin to understand, but that pulled on my heart-strings at every move.

Dawn over Agra! The first red arc of sun broke over the horizon, the muezzin called and the city stirred rapidly from sleep. Raucous parakeets, green and long-tailed, swooped excitedly from tree to tree, revealing flashes of iridescent blue wings in their frantic flight.

The intense sun resembled a burning ball floating mysteriously in the mist above a dusty town thrown suddenly into life. Below in the narrow streets tiny shops had dark interiors, bright lights flashed on brass scales, small boys sat cross-legged among rice and lentils, pigs foraged, cows meandered, and traders sought the shade of trees. From a jumble of houses and tumbling bricks, small girls in pristine white dresses and smart red cardigans emerged to pile into rickshaws for the school run.

Agra to me meant the Taj Mahal, the greatest monument to love. Built by Shah Jahan in memory of his beloved wife Mumtaz Mahal who died in childbirth in 1629, it is the perfect Mogul garden tomb.

Nothing could have prepared me for its beauty. None of my photographs could ever do it justice, capture the iridescence of marble, show the exquisite detail of carvings or the intensity of the inlays. It is, perhaps, the most wonderful sight in world.

Next, as a sightseer, I travelled to Old Delhi with its crowded narrow streets and its remarkable Red Fort; and New Delhi, the administrative capital with its tree-lined avenues and elegant buildings designed by Sir Edwin Lutyens and Sir Herbert Baker.

Driving anywhere in India is a revelation, the roads a tangle of hot metal, a cacophanous jungle of lorries, buses and cabs, trishaws, scooters and bicycles, and cows that wander at will through it all, somehow surviving all noxious fumes that emanate from a forest of exhausts. 'Hoot please!' exhorted signs on the back of every lorry and truck—a request happily adhered to by all drivers!

On the rural roads briskly trotting horses pulled carts, overburdened donkeys plodded along and ponderous oxen pulled their loads amid elderly tractors, battered buses billowed black smoke, and bone-rattling bicycles were ridden in single file and at a stately pace.

Travelling to Jaipur revealed another mode of transport—camels. Not my favourite! Goats nibbled delicately at low growing bushes, cows wallowed in a muddy lake and pointy-nosed pigs scampered across roads in a flurry of trotters.

Gangling eucalyptus, tall pampas grass and flat-topped acacias grew in the dry, sandy soil where the oxen dragged home-made ploughs; roadside villages sprang suddenly into abundant colour as women in saris of luminous hue went about their daily tasks.

Jaipur was fascinating and chaotic, a people-packed trading city of constant clamour and vibrant colour. There were broad avenues and narrow passageways, a honeycomb of tiny shops, their wares expressing the cultural diversities of India, where gold glistened, lingering spices and heady perfumes scented the air and young boys could be seen on dusty roadsides deftly stripping engines.

It was time to travel to Bombay. A delayed flight resulted in a night view of Bombay—tall buildings, bright lights and still undimmed street life.

Looking up at the clock-tower I realised that I had arrived at my rendezvous many hours too early and that there was plenty of time to see some of the sights of Bombay before meeting the Mission's representative. There was no shortage of self-appointed guides to show me the tourist attraction 'Gateway to India'—a magnificent edifice, but only a gateway to those coming in from the beach.

'Would you like your photograph taken, mem sahib?' asked the 'con' man as he put his little monkey on my shoulder and pocketed the half rupee that he said it would cost. I never saw him again, nor the photograph!

All the sights and sounds were a novelty to me, not to mention the smell of people and the aroma of curries at the little stalls by the roadside. Anything from a shave to a shoe-shine to a massage would be performed out of doors and witnessed by the curious bystanders who hung around.

The ever present crowd of children begging made it very difficult to find solitude, and so it was not without difficulty that I eventually found an unoccupied seat where I was able to write the postcards and letters that would let the praying people back home know that I had arrived in India.

The ride on a bicycle taxi was a hair raising experience as the driver gave me the impression that he owned the road. Motor traffic was ignored as he swerved and manoeuvred in between cars, bullock carts and pedestrians. He had, however, a respect for traffic lights and it was comforting to know that he recognised the red light as a sign to stop! Whenever he did stop the little brown faces appeared at the sides of the taxi and the outstretched arms of children seemed to be everywhere.

'Money, mem sahib, money!', was a cry that was hard to resist. I once gave a beggar child a whole rupee without realising the folly of such an action. Suddenly, I was surrounded by many professional beggar children who were very difficult to shake off.

The need to change my European dresses for Indian saris dawned upon me following a very embarrassing incident when one little child peeped up my skirt to see if I was white all over! She disappeared as quickly as she came—her eyes the size of prunes and her teeth as white as snow against her dark skin when she grinned at me!

Bombay has a good selection of splendid hotels and I saw them during my tour, yet it was not until I walked down a side street which led behind those big hotels that I experienced such a cultural shock. Down these streets the poor people were living in disgustingly filthy shacks. There was evidence of poverty and dirt all around. The stench of sewerage mingled with the smell of curry. Dirty faced children were sitting outside on the ground eating bowls of rice. Some worn-out mothers were trying to bathe their naked, pot-bellied children by standing them in aluminium bowls and washing them down. Others were trying to feed their screaming babies, some of whom were dying from malnutrition and diarrhoea.

So much wealth was around the corner where the smart hotels were standing, but extreme poverty existed in the back streets. In some streets emaciated bodies were left to die. Flies were all over them and they were too weak to swish them away. Many were either the very old or the very young. As for the children, the parents found it hard to feed them, for they had already many mouths to feed, and so some little ones were invariably abandoned.

The sight of young children left to die at the end of a platform in the Railway Station, with a piece of sacking as their only early possessions, was distressing. What a contrast between the breathtaking view of the Taj Mahal and the first horrific glimpse of the underworld of poverty and suffering that is probably the real India.

I went to Bombay Railway Station to meet my senior missionary and to collect my luggage.There was my large blue trunk awaiting me which I had sent on ahead. It was mostly full of books which made it extremely heavy and I could not move it even an inch. I asked the porters if they would carry it for me.

'Oh, no, missy, this is hernia trunk!' came the reply.

Suddenly, I was aware of a white skinned lady dressed in a pretty sari standing beside me. Her long blonde hair was plaited and fastened into a coronet style around her head. She put her hand on my shoulder. Having heard the comments about the hernia trunk there was laughter in her deep blue eyes.

'G'day, you must be Janice,' she said, giving me a welcoming hug. 'I'm Claire Decker. I'm so pleased to see you. Welcome to India, my dear, and may God richly use you during your time here.'

We spent a short time together, allowing me to complete my sight-seeing in hot and humid Bombay. The great bougainvillaea arches and the exotic eastern colours stay in my memory to this day.

The time with Claire passed quickly by as we shared experiences. Her eyes nearly popped out of her head when she discovered I'd come overland with six Australian men. More important than that, I learned from her a little of the reality of being a missionary in India.

Refreshed by a cup of tea at a roadside cafe, we made our way to the Mission's old Land Rover, parked outside the railway station. The eastern sun made the inside of the vehicle unbearably hot and I longed for a cool breeze as we made the dusty trip to the Mission station.

The nearer I was to the Mission the more I felt as if I was really going to Siberia.

'It's too hot for Siberia,' Claire chuckled as we bumped along, manoeuvering around a bullock cart and avoiding yet another white sacred cow who seemed to think India was hers.

'Well, Janice, here we are,' declared Claire as she stopped to open the rusty old gates that led into the Mission's compound.

MEDITATION

> There is no coldness, Lord, in Thee,
> O keep us kindled, lest we bring
> To our dear Lord of Calvary
> Dead ashes for our offering.

Amy Carmichael

CHAPTER SIXTEEN

A Missionary at Last

"Come, follow me," Jesus said,
"and I will make you fishers of men."
(Mark 1:17)

DURING the long, hot, dusty drive from Bombay to the Western Ghats, Claire Decker told me many things about life on a mission station and I built up a mental picture of what I should see once the orientation course was completed.

It was not a bit as I imagined it! The shabby mission buildings, which included the hospital, were much bigger than I supposed. Claire introduced me to the other missionaries—a team of five women who were responsiblefor the running of the mission They were fluent in the language and extremely experienced in the work. However, they looked very weary from almost constantly working in the intense Indian heat. Nevertheless, they put by time to welcome me, which included a special Indian meal. A little later I was to see them again in different parts of the mission, busy in the work to which I felt God had called me.

Claire took me to my quarters and gave me a couple of days to settle in before showing me around.

I do not know to this day how my 'hernia trunk' arrived there! Claire must have had more influence over the porters in Bombay than I, and someone else must have carried it from a bullock cart to my room, but surely not the slight, but willing, houseboy who hovered around! I opened the blue, sturdy trunk and there were my precious books, safe and sound. I never feel at home until I have unpacked my books and arranged them on shelves in a way that meets with my approval.

Anna and John, who had occupied the room previously, kindly left behind their book shelves when they packed to go on a furlough, so there was no delay in settling in.

My western clothing was packed away in the now empty trunk and I began to wear my new saris. There is a certain technique to belearned of wrapping, folding and tucking in a sari before throwing the long end over one's shoulder. At the beginning, I did not always do it with the expertise that I acquired later on, and there was an embarrassing moment, witnessed by the houseboy, when my sari fell off! The little Indian girl in Bombay who peeped up my western skirt only grinned—the houseboy did not spare my blushes—he laughed loudly, shouting, 'Oh, golly gosh! Look at Miss Janice. Oh, golly gosh!'

Among my belongings there was a crocheted cloth lovingly made by one of my Christian friends as a present for me. I placed it over the blue trunk which was positioned under the window in my room. It looked very attractive.

Yes, I thought, this it is may be India, but it is also now my home. I want my room to look nice.

The presence of Claire outside my door reminded me that it was time to look around and see the work that was going on in the mission.

'In our village,' Claire explained, 'the natural water contains excessive fluoride that, along with vitamin deficiency, causes bad discoloration of the teeth, especially in the five to six year olds. In an area like ours, where malnutrition is a big problem, it is difficult to isolate any one particular cause and there is very little we can do to help them. Oh, Janice, how desperately we need a dentist out here. We must make it a matter of prayer that God will send us one—one who will live by faith.'

We walked across to the paediatric ward of the little mission hospital. There we saw children with swollen bellies, vitamin deficiency, eye complaints and pulmonary disease. Those little ones in care were the fortunate ones. There was a multitude of similar cases in the world outside who would receive no treatment. Claire, a paediatric trained nurse, was longing for the day when, not only a Christian dentist would come, but a Christian doctor would join the team to supervise both the medical and surgical side of the Mission's work.

'We need an on-going supply of drugs,' explained Claire, shaking her head. 'In fact, we're constantly out of most things, aren't we?'

We called in at the Common Room for a cup of tea. After our tour in such intense heat I wanted a drink so much and I was beginning to wonder if I would ever get one. It was with a sigh of relief that I sank into an old but comfortable chair and reached for a cup of stewed tea, offered to me by the still chuckling house-boy.

Zilda, our senior nurse, said she would show me around the rest of the mission station. However, when the time came she was too busy, so Claire continued the tour.

'We haven't a laboratory technician,' Claire told me, 'And I don't know what he or she would make of this if we had one. Our laboratory is so badly equipped.'

'In what way?' I asked.

'Well, look for yourself! Look at the stuff that we have and there is no technical back-up here. We were given this blood gas analiser using radio isotopes. It's obviously useless.'

I liked Claire very much. I felt comfortable with her. There was such a frankness about her. Most missionaries seem to be 'thankful' for everything, including the useless, but not Claire. She said exactly what she thought.

Jenny, another nurse, who had been in India for only about a year, joined us. The three of us strolled across to the 'Special Nutritional Centre and Rest Home' for the elderly, the young mothers and the malnourished children.

'It's here that we supervise their recuperation,' said Jenny, obviously feeling the heat—she mopped perspiration from her brow and the back of her neck with the end of her sari.

Before we entered the 'Centre' we were overtaken by some youngsters on callipers and crutches. They were a happy group and seemed to be managing wonderfully well in spite of their limitations.

'The immunisation programme came too late for some,' said Claire.

'Our area was involved in a polio epidemic and there was no protection, but those kids who have suffered seem to cope very well,' Jenny smiled towards them lovingly.

At the end of the tour and a hot, sticky day I was glad to retire to my room. That room, which was to be my home, was also home to bugs, beetles, fleas, lice, flies and mosquitoes and I put up a real fight to keep them at bay. When I lit my smelly little paraffin lamp and tried to read the moths became a real nuisance. They would see the light of the lamp and come circling and fluttering around it. I arranged to have rigged up a central light with a bowl of water under it. The moths, seeing the reflection of the light in the water, drowned. Well, some of them did. The others were smashed to dust by me at an alarming rate!

Before retiring to bed on my first night the houseboy brought me a mosquito net and a *very* sharp knife, similar to the kind seen in an English butcher's shop. The knife was always kept within reach in case a snake or a rat invaded the room. During my years in India I thankfully never needed to use my knife, although other members in our team did. Zilda, our senior missionary nurse, awoke early one morning to find a snake curled up beside her. With great presence of mind, she slowly reached for her knife and, with one swift movement, cut the snake into pieces. The worst moment in the whole episode was when it was served up in a soup for the evening meal!

MEDITATION

I once heard the story of a young boy who was standing at a dockyard, watching barrels of molasses being loaded. Suddenly one barrel swung over him and burst open. The sticky substance fell all over him and, for the first time in his life, he prayed, 'Oh, Lord, give me a tongue worthy of the task!'

Oh, Lord, make me worthy of the task you have set before me.

CHAPTER SEVENTEEN

Much to Learn

'DOCTOR! DOCTOR!' someone shouted, banging loudly on my door.

I have never been very good at getting up once having retired to bed, but this time there was no choice—the banging was not going to stop.

I slipped on my long, pink, cotton dressing gown and brown leather sandals. I rubbed my eyes, trying hard to shake off the feeling of sleepiness.

'Who are you? What do you want?' I shouted back through my door.

'Hurry, please, doctor,' pleaded a man's voice.

'I am NOT a doctor,' I said slowly, 'I am a missionary—a nurse and a midwife.'

'You must come, doctor,' shouted the man, who was still banging on my door.

As I gingerly opened the badly fitting door, a strong, dark, hairy hand quickly gripped my arm.

'Girl much sick!' shouted his companion.

I grabbed my medical bag and flash light and went off with the two strangers. They half dragged me out through the compound's gates and pushed me along the dark narrow streets. I was taken to a wooden shack with a corrugated iron roof upon which the moonlight shone.

Inside was a girl of about thirteen or fourteen years of age.

'What is the matter with her?' I asked in my new

language, shining my flashlight into the darkness of the squalid, cramped room.

Quickly they told me her story. At the age of twelve years this girl was sold to the priests in the Temple for prostitution and, after a year with them, she became pregnant. The baby, now ready to be born, was coming feet first instead of head first—a delivery that is not always easy in an ideal western setting, let alone in a remote Indian village. The most senior woman in the village declared herself an 'expert midwife'. When the baby's foot appeared, this self appointed 'expert' said that it was 'of a devil' and promptly cut off the baby's little limb, leaving one dead infant still not born. The young mother was grossly dehydrated and very close to death. Moving her could put her into further shock and cause her to die. I had to take a chance for I could do nothing for her in such dark, unhygienic conditions. I requested that the men carry the young girl to our inadequately stocked 'delivery suite' at the Mission Station There was so much blood everywhere—hers and the baby's and I needed to be able to examine her properly in a very good light. They shook their heads because those Asian men rarely went near women in labour.

'DO IT **NOW**!' I commanded at the top of my voice, stamping my foot. It was done, but not without a lot of verbal abuse from them. We hurried back along the dark narrow streets and through the rusty compound's gates with a much greater sense of urgency than the men who sought my assistance a little time before.

The 'delivery suite' was very different from the clinically clean and well equipped one in the east London hospital where I trained as a midwife. The floor in our mission's 'delivery suite' was a dirt one with a covering of manure mixed with tea leaves! The mixture was effective as a dust controller but, oh, the smell!

The frail little body of the girl was placed on the delivery table.

The other missionaries turned out of their beds to assist me—Joy, a *teacher* (!), and the other Claire, a paediatric trained nurse. The young houseboy also helped by swishing any flying bugs away from the patient.

A little gauze mask was placed over the girl's face by one of my 'assistants' and the smell of chloroform began to pervade the place, nullifying a little the smell of the manure.

On examination I discovered that the dead baby's shoulders were stuck.

'Oh, what a mess! I will have to crush the shoulders in order to get this baby out…', I began.

'Janice, forget it. She's gone,' Claire interrupted, a sadness in her voice.

The young mother's life had slipped away.

From the day of her birth until the moment she passed beyond human help she was part of a way of life with nothing to commend it. I failed to save her. I was saddened even further by the realisation that the opportunity never came to tell her of Jesus, the sinner's friend. And now it was too late.

I went outside the building to tell the news to the villagers who were noisily crowding around outside the compound. News seemed to travel fast in our village! Although we had made many friends amongst the people who lived in our remote village, there were also those who were eager to stir up trouble for the Mission. We were disliked by all of the Hindu holy men and the minority of Muslims in the community were very hostile towards us. The situation could have turned nasty at that stage.

'This foreigner is not a doctor,' shouted one man, angrily. 'She's a fake!'

I was thankful that I learned their language back in

England and was able, with a fair amount of fluency, to explain to them what happened. It was a real relief that there was no violent disturbance.

'May God have mercy on your souls,' I said, raising my right hand.

The crowd began to disperse at the call of another woman who removed any remaining tension by turning to the crowd and saying,

'Never mind. Come away. What is all this fuss about? The dead girl was a nothing anyway. Who cares?'

Sickness, death, helplessness to save the body, difficulties in communicating the gospel to hostile people in order to save their souls, so that one watched body and soul pass into darkness from which there is no return. The need! Oh, the need!

Next morning, Zilda, our senior missionary came to see me in my room about the events of the night before. She sat on my bed and, in a manner that did not arouse any ill feeling whatever, gently reprimanded me about the way I reacted to the urgent summons from outside my bedroom.

'I realise that you are new to life out here, Janice,' she said, 'I appreciate your motives and what you did to try and save that young mother's life, but never leave the Mission compound at night on your own. If you have to go out then get someone else up to go with you. OK?

She went on to explain that it might not have been a genuine call for help at all, and to go outside the compound at night in the company of two unknown men was sheer folly. She told me that it was not unknown for people to go missing in India and she did not want anything like that to happen to me.

I realised there was much for me to learn about many things. However, one thing was quite certain—I was a missionary at last!

CHRISTIAN COUNSEL

Before my departure for India Mrs Lloyd-Jones stopped me one Sunday afternoon and gave me this advice:

'There'll be hard times when Satan will try and persuade you that you shouldn't be a missionary. But you must have none of it. You just quote Scripture and tell the Devil, 'I am doing a great work so that I cannot come down: why should the work cease whilst I leave it, and come down to you?' (Nehemiah 6:3 AV)

CHAPTER EIGHTEEN

Women Only

> 'There were also many women there... who had followed Jesus from Galilee ministering to him.'
> (Matthew 27:55, RSV)

THE company of those six Australian men on the journey to Asia was in strange contrast to the company of my five missionary colleagues who were all women. Sometimes, on the journey to the East, situations arose which called for the kind of physical strength that is usually the possession of many men, but few women. Driving over difficult terrain, changing wheels on the Land Rover or moving boulders from the roadway was something that the Australians took in their stride. MEN'S WORK! I played my part by doing some driving, cooking meals or acting as the group's medical adviser, but it was a comfort to know that there were men around.

The five women at the Mission station were a strong team. Attractive, slim and feminine they nevertheless taught themselves to do what some would call 'men's work'. Wheels on the Land Rover were changed with zeal and dexterity, heavy boulders were somehow moved aside on the unmade roads of rural India and, when the road ran out and the Land Rover could go no further, they would hoist up their saris to knee level and tramp across the rough fields to visit farmers who may have contracted leprosy.

I became the sixth member of this female team, sharing in the work and ministry of the Christian church. Although there were men on other Mission stations, we had no male member to help us and there was work to be done which is considered by some Church leaders to be the task of MEN ONLY.

In the absence of male workers, there is only one alternative to leaving the work undone and that is to go ahead and do it!

Whenever Christians gather together to celebrate the Breaking of Bread, the Lord's Supper, the Holy Communion, or whatever other name they choose to call it, the sex of the celebrant is a thorny issue. Whenever our Field Superintendent decided to pay us a visit we assumed, quite naturally, that he would lead the worship, preach the Word of God and officiate at the Lord's Table. It was good to have this man around, but his visits were only occasional—about twice a year. Most days we gathered together in the evening to hear the words, 'Do this in remembrance of me,' and to break bread together in the presence of our risen Lord. On these occasions Zilda, our senior lady missionary, would take over the leadership of our gatherings and bring the elements to us.

On a Sunday morning Indian Christians were made welcome at the service and, providing they were true believers, they were invited to share in the Breaking of Bread. On these occasions we took it in turns to officiate and did not feel that we were trespassing in a sphere of ministry that should be labelled MEN ONLY.

We practised only one mode of baptism and that was by immersion in the river. In Hindu society baptism is seen as a decisive step and is only performed when someone makes a profession of conversion, showing evidence that they are Christian disciples by openly destroying their Hindu idols. Only then are they considered candidates for baptism. The destroying of Hindu idols can arouse fierce opposition from the immediate family of a convert. His brothers in fact put one of the men I baptised in the river to death. There were no witnesses, but it was thought that he was knocked on the head, ferried out into the river in a small rowing boat and thrown overboard.

During my stay at the Mission station I witnessed about thirty baptisms in the river and the women performed all of these, with the exception of one. On this occasion the baptismal service coincided with the visit of the Field Superintendent and he, naturally, took over.

Baptising by immersion calls for a certain amount of physical strength and could be considered MEN'S WORK. In some baptisms in the Western world when the candidate is a hefty man or buxom woman I have seen two men carry out the immersion so that they had the united strength to lift the new convert back out of the water. In poor Indian villages overweight persons are hardly ever seen, so candidates for baptism were usually thin, wiry people. Some of the stronger women taking a baptismal service could cope on their own. It is a thrilling sound to hear the words ring out over the river bank, 'On confession of your faith in the Lord Jesus Christ, I baptise you in the name of the Father, the Son and Holy Spirit'.

There was no indigenous church exactly where we were. There certainly was in many other parts of India for years and years before, and with national and international structures. However, our Mission was an interdenominational faith Mission and so we formed our own little Bible-based chapel for the new Christians. Its human leadership? The women, of course!

In 1947 India was given her independence and the British presence was slowly disappearing. We wondered what the future held for missionary societies and ours in particular. Would the time come when missionaries would be withdrawn from India just as they had been from the great land of China? Some members of our Mission experienced difficulty in getting their visas renewed and this led us to think that our days there could be numbered. We already realised how important it was to train workers from the ranks of the local Christians. One of our team was very gifted in training Bible-women. She trained herself to sit cross-legged on the ground for long periods of time so that she could instruct them without too much discomfort.

It was a great day when a well-educated Christian believer moved into our locality. He was a high caste Hindu who had moved away from another town because of hostility from his family and, together with his wife, he took up residence in a house near the mission station. He was fluent in English and offered his services to the Mission. It soon became apparent that this man showed the makings of a good Christian Indian pastor, but how could we train him? What did the Apostle Paul mean when he wrote to Timothy*, 'permit no woman to teach or have authority over men; she is to keep silent'? Whatever the interpretation we realised that we must do something.

We arranged a correspondence course with a Bible Institute in the United Kingdom which was very helpful. Even so, he needed the help of our lady missionaries in working his way through the course. He gained practical experience in communicating the Gospel when he came with us to our open-air evangelistic outreach meetings during the Hindu festivals and also amongst the crowds in the local bazaar.

We played Gospel records on an old wind up gramophone and joined in the singing ourselves. This 'noise' always attracted curious on-lookers. The Hindus

---

* See 1 Timothy 2:12

enjoy music but they did not always interpret the words as one intended them to be understood! An example of this was when I was singing along with a Gospel hymn which said, 'Bring me water, water, the water of life' without realising that the words could be interpreted literally. I became aware of this when the record was being played to a queue of out-patients at the clinic. Then some well-intentioned Hindu women took their pitchers to the river and brought me water!

Our Indian helper was able to get the message across without being misunderstood in this way, his command of the language being a very real advantage. Opportunities to preach in the Sunday services were given to him and our fellowship of lady missionaries rejoiced to know they were playing some part in the steady development of this man into a fully accredited pastor.

Dressed in 'best clothes', missionaries from the different mission stations met together in a nearby town for the Indian man's ordination service. The Field Superintendent presided over the gathering and, in an atmosphere of worship and thanksgiving, we felt so glad that, whatever the future held for our Mission, a real move had been made towards a strong indigenous Christian church.

JUST A THOUGHT

Why is it assumed that women are only called to the mission field because there is a shortage of men? Could it not be that in certain circumstances a woman is God's first choice? There isn't a man living who could have done what Gladys Aylward did in China.

CHAPTER NINETEEN

That Dreaded Disease

'A man with leprosy came to him [i.e. Jesus] and begged him on his knees, "If you are willing, you can make me clean."' (Mark 1:40)

DURING my second year in India, the Missionary Society arranged for me to be sent to Vellore Hospital in the south of India, where I engaged in an intensive course on all aspects of leprosy. This gave me enough medical experience to be appointed as one of the Indian government's leprosy workers in Maharashtra. It was part of my work to have the gratifying privilege of issuing to former leprosy patients an all important certificate stating that they were free from the disease. Naturally one never used the word 'clean' as in New Testament times, but to be declared free from it was a happy experience for them. In practice, however, the Certificate of Health was not always acknowledged. So great is the stigma surrounding leprosy that ignorant folk follow the maxim 'once a leper, always a leper'. Because of their disfigurement, they were regarded as still having the disease, which meant that they could not ride on public transport or meet in public places.

The crack of dawn heralded the start of our working day. I marvel that I used to get out of bed at the unsociable hour of 4.45 a.m. to contact the farmers in their fields at around 6 a.m. After a cup of tea and a cookie, an Indian worker and I would climb up into the decrepit old Land

Rover and bump our way over the unmade roads to a location as near to the farmer's field as possible. We'd wave to him and, more often than not, he would drop what he was doing and come over to meet us. My leprosy detection work was performed in conjunction with the Indian Health Authority; it was to them I had to send the medical records along with my reports. Only very occasionally did I have to pull rank and tell a farmer that, if he did not comply with Government policy, I would have to bring out an official to see him. On the whole there was a willingness to be examined for the early signs of the skin disease. I would examine for the first indication of leprosy, displaying itself by a slight thickening of the skin on parts of the face and ears with a loss of the outer portions of the eyebrows; there were also faint pigmentary changes in the skin. Contacting the farmers gave us the golden opportunity of telling them and their families about the love of the Lord Jesus Christ.

When the signs of the disease were in evidence it was necessary to go to the man's home to examine his wife and family. This again opened the way to tell of the One who loved them so much that he gave his only Son, that if they believed in him, they'd have eternal life.

Their babies are not born with the disease, yet living in such close contact with those who had leprosy meant that, sooner or later, they were likely to contract the disease.

The medication I administered to my patients, suffering from leprosy, was highly effective, yet the side effects made some people feel very poorly. In a small hospital, not much bigger than a three or four bedroomed house, about ten miles from our little Mission I was, in the absence of a doctor, in sole charge of a twenty bedded ward. The ward was reserved for those patients who couldn't cope with the side effects of Diamino-diphenylsulphone (DDS), the only drug we had to deal with the disease.

I forbade them, however, to bring in idols, Hindu or otherwise. As a Christian missionary, I enforced a strict policy of no compromise.

Whenever we missionaries were due for a vacation we were usually encouraged to spend it at another Mission Station. The Mission Field Superintendent who was based several thousand miles away wired to say it was my turn to have six weeks off and would I like to go to the Seychelles again. I was tempted, but I chose to spend it down in Madras where our oldest active field worker was living. She never let on about her age, but she was into her sixties.

A small rotund woman, she was a mother in Israel to many new recruits. Known as Auntie Cee to all our Christian workers, she was loved by us all.

I'd heard it said that one knows nothing about India until having travelled on a train. My journey to Madras, therefore, had to be by rail. Some such journeys can take days; this one I remember well. The sun was high as the train clattered through the red fields on its way to the South.

The compartment had filled up during the night of the journey. A fat grandmother had spread herself on the seat opposite. An old lanky man with a long, black moustache snored loudly in the luggage rack above. Then from down the corridor a new noise started up. Two children appeared—a little boy with a huge accordian hanging from his neck, and his sister. The girl shut her eyes, tossed back her head and sang, 'You are my sunshine, my only sunshine', while doing a sort of dance in the narrow corridor. When the song finished she went around the compartment holding out her hand for money.

'Shoo! shoo! Go away!' said the fat grandmother.

The little girl stuck out her tongue and the two scampered off down the corridor with wicked grins on their faces.

The train began to slow down. A small station was approaching—really just a local stop. Still there was plenty going on—people coming and going.

I jumped down on to the platform, taking a water bottle with me. A man with a cart piled high with soft drinks pushed his way through the crowd calling out the prices in a sing song voice. I was just putting on the cap of the water bottle at the drinking fountain when the station-master clanged his bell, the guard flapped his flag, the train jerked into action and started moving slowly off. I broke into a run and hopped on to the foot plate at the very last minute.

After that excitement a man came round selling tea from a huge tea-pot. He was followed by a young girl selling sprays of jasmine for the hair. The fat grandmother wanted the jasmine. I asked for tea. Soon the tiny compartment was as busy and as bustling as the station itself.

Finally, it settled down again to the clickerty-clack music of the train wheels. A white shrine in a field flashed past. A line of white birds slept on the telegraph wires between the poles. A group of children and a man with a bicycle waved from the barrier of a level crossing. They were there and then they were gone.

The train carried me to the station I had been waiting for, where I had to change trains. There were people selling things and passengers chasing porters who ran ahead with luggage perilously perched on their heads.

However, above all the noise and the hubbub there came from the end of the platform a hiss of steam and a long, high whistle that shook the birds out of the sky. The air became hotter and the steam cleared. There stood before me the most magnificent steam engine I had ever seen. The engine driver leaned out of his cab.

'Hey! I have to change here. Are you going to Madras?' I called.

'You had better climb aboard because steam trains don't wait for anyone—not even you, mem sahib!' he yelled back, giving me a big wink.

It was wonderful for me to finally reach Madras and be in the company of dear Auntie Cee. There was so much to say for we had not seen each other for well over a year and she wanted to catch up on all my news and what was going on in the area where I worked. It was lovely to have fellowship and prayer with that dear old saint.

Next morning, when we sat together at breakfast, I asked if I could wander around Madras.

'I am a little too weary to take you sight-seeing. Are you able to go without me, dear? I'll send one of our reliable Indian Christian workers with you so that you will not be completely alone. OK?' she said. I agreed and my Indian companion and I set off together to see where East meets West. It may now be the film capital, the Hollywood of South India, but colourful Madras, an amalgam of modern industry and ancient culture, established in 1639 as the British East India Company's first trading station on the east coast, still had many recognisably British buildings. They were laced by wide roads of fast moving traffic and tiny, narrow backstreets teeming with vibrant life. Men wore white dhotis or lungis, and women moved gracefully in saris of brilliant contrasting colours in a climate that went from hot to hotter. Palm and casuarina trees edged the mile long marina, an esplanade where university colleges, and a circular Victorian ice factory, faced out over a wide beach and the calmly lapping Bay of Bengal.

Although a stronghold of Hindu culture and tradition, I was amazed to discover that Madras had quite a large Christian population, witnessed by the many churches in daily use. How unlike the remote village where I was stationed.

'You must be tired after all that sightseeing. Come and have some tea with me,' said the elderly missionary.

I sat down at the table. Sitting opposite this white-haired lady and chatting to her, it slowly dawned upon me that something was not quite right. The outer parts of her eyebrows were missing.

At no time during my leprosy work was I afraid of the disease. It never occurred to me that any member of the Mission would contract it, but I was now mistaken.

Breaking it to her as gently as I could, she gave me permission to give her a check-up. Sure enough, there was the evidence. She was a leper. Fortunately, the 'dreaded disease' was not so advanced that there was loss of sensation in her hands or feet. However, it was the end of an outstanding missionary career. She never wanted to leave the India she loved, but there was no other alternative. The Field Superintendent was informed.

Auntie Cee was started on a course of DDS tablets whilst arrangements were made for her reluctant return to the United Kingdom. After receiving intensive treatment at the Hospital for Tropical Diseases in London she then was transferred to a home in Suffolk for retired missionaries. She never saw her beloved India again, but she's in a far better place now—Auntie Cee is with the Lord in heaven.

MEDITATION

> Into the love of God, I pray,
> Deeper and deeper let me press.

CHAPTER TWENTY

Visa Refused

I worked very hard for almost four years, heavily engaged in evangelism and midwifery, but mostly leprosy work, on the hot and dusty plains of Western India. Then I was taken ill.

Bob Jones, the Mission's Superintendent considered a rest up in the Nilgiri Hills, where the vegetation was lush and the air fresher; he claimed it would do me the world of good. Bob arranged for Dr. David Henry, an Anglo-Indian Christian, to visit me there. Dr. Henry diagnosed severe amoebic dysentery, bacillary dysentery and hepatitis 'A'. Complications had arisen which were affecting my body's vital organs, the lungs in particular.

'She could be treated in Bombay, probably quite successfully,' Dr. Henry declared.

'Probably? What do you mean by probably? Oh, no. This particular Mission holds the firm policy never to take any risks with a missionary's health. Janice is only a few months away from her first furlough, so I think we'd be wise to send her home. She'll have the best of care in London.'

Dr. Henry didn't agree. He believed I should be treated in India, in Bombay, and then I'd be fit to enjoy my furlough. But Bob was adamant.

My physical condition rapidly worsened. I was flown to Heathrow and rushed as an emergency to the Hospital for Tropical Diseases in St. Pancras.

I was hospitalised for quite some time, undergoing tests and being subjected to nasty treatments, making me feel even weaker.

My main objective was to get well, have done with my furlough and return to India—the land I'd not only come to love, but to regard as my home. No longer were the Indian people foreign to me with strange customs, language and food. I didn't care about hardship or even ridicule; they were family and I desperately wanted to rejoin them and continue with my ministry. With me there was an all-or-nothingness about the things that I desired for India. I couldn't ask it from others—it had to begin with me, something living and dynamic.

However, I was not coping with the way the illness, along with the sheer fatigue accompanying it, was affecting me spiritually. I suppose, like many other Christians, I did not fully understand the interplay of body, mind and spirit which made for good health. It seemed, at the time, to be just a spiritual low and I tried, in vain, to deal with it as such.

I called to God but my prayers seemed to ascend no higher than the ceiling of the hospital ward. I needed to experience his presence. Perhaps the Psalmist felt like this when he penned: 'Why are you down cast, O my soul? Why are you so disturbed within me? (Psalm 42:5). No apparent answer came and prayer began to seem like a waste of time. I was being nursed in isolation and I was conscious of the comings and goings of doctors and nurses, but the sense of God's presence, so precious to a Christian, was absent.

I am, by nature, a fairly private person and I do not find it easy to confide in other people. Nevertheless, I plucked up sufficient courage to send a message to a minister acquaintance of mine, requesting a visit. My message arrived at the manse at a time when he was just leaving for a conference.

My whereabouts in London were obviously known to all the staff at the Mission's home base in London but, for some reason, no-one visited me. Maybe they thought that they might catch something.

Not expecting anyone during the afternoon's visiting time, I decided to have forty-winks.

'Janice, wake up, you've a visitor,' said the Ward Sister, giving my shoulder a gentle shake.

I rubbed my eyes. There, standing by my bed in a white mask and green gown, was Helen. (She and I shared a room together during our student days.)

My eyes widened. 'What are you doing here?' I happily enquired, propping myself up a little in the hospital bed.

Fussing around me and plumping up my pillows before sitting down beside my bed, she told me how she'd read in the Mission's newsletter that I was ill in hospital. Helen peered at me over her mask. 'You do look a mess. My word, you look an awful mess. Look at your hair. And you're so jaundiced,' she continued bluntly. 'You've turned from a grape to a raisin.'

'Gee, thanks. All these compliments ... I feel a whole load better now!' I said, sarcastically. Then I explained all that happened to me.

'Well, my friend, I am going to take you in hand from the moment you are discharged,' she said firmly.

Taking a small phial of perfume from her handbag she sprayed my wrists with the expensive aroma. 'That'll make you feel good. I mean it... you're coming to stay with us... and it's no good shaking your head.'

'Look, Helen, I do appreciate all your good intentions, but as soon as I am better... well, I'll be able to sort myself out and return to India. So, don't worry about me, darling,' I said. 'I'm a tougher old bird than I may seem right now.' Being Helen, she took little or no notice.

When I was finally discharged from the hospital, Helen

insisted I spent my convalescent time with her and her family.

On my hurried return to England, the sum total of the clothing I had packed consisted of a couple of saris, three nighties, some underwear and a pair of worn out sandals. I'd left the rest of my belongings in my room at the Mission in India, ready for my return.

Helen, staring at me like some waif from the third world, dragged me along to Marks and Spencers in Croydon. There she kitted me out with western fashions. It was strange to be in such dress after so long. With all those collars, buttons, zips, belts and tights, I felt like a trussed-up chicken!

One never to be forgotten day, whilst I was still staying with Helen, the postman dropped through a letter from the Indian Embassy. Eagerly, I ripped open the envelope, knowing it had to be something to do with my visa. India, here I come, I thought, but my heart sank as I read that my visa application had been refused.

Trudging to my room, I caught sight of my reflection in a large mirror and, staring back at myself, began to think about that vast continent of India. It seemed only like yesterday that, as the Mission's newest recruit, I'd been overwhelmed by the enormity of the work. Yet, I had packed so much into those years—failures and successes, tragedies and blessings.

My thoughts were interrupted by Helen. 'Janice, come on down and join us,' she called. 'There's someone here who is anxious to meet you.'

'May I introduce Mrs Belle Yates, our pastor's mother. Mrs Yates is visiting her son and his wife here in Sutton, just for a couple of weeks,' Theo, Helen's husband, informed me.

I shook hands with this smartly dressed, elderly woman and then sat down beside her on the squashy settee. Helen had disappeared into the kitchen to make coffee.

I smiled at the visitor. 'Where do you come from?' I asked. 'I can't place the accent.'

'Oh, I come from Nottingham. After my husband's death, two years ago, I thought about retiring into a little bungalow in Worthing, but I stayed put. I'd had too many good memories to leave behind. I belong there. Anyway, I hear you're a missionary. Do tell me…'

I didn't feel like telling anyone anything at that point; but this woman was plying me with questions, about my furlough, and so on. 'No. It seems that I'm not to be a missionary anymore.' I felt sick at heart and I certainly wasn't ready to talk about what had come in the post. Yet she was a forward, persistent woman.

'I've been in India for… um… almost four years, a full term, but I came home a bit early because of some bugs I picked up out there. I expect Helen and Theo have told you. I heard only this morning that my visa has been refused, so I can't return. I dunno why, as the need for missionaries is just as great now as ever it was.'

I hoped the topic of conversation would change, yet she continued. 'My dear Janice, were you sure you were really meant to be in India in the first place?'

'Why?' I asked.

'Well, it wasn't very long, and now with no visa…'

She was wrong. I knew that my call had been definite and clear. Yet what was happening in my experience now was anything but clear.

It was a joy for Helen and me to meet Janette in London. She was a fellow missionary who was also home on furlough, yet from another mission station. The three of us went for something to eat at the *Golden Egg*, just along from Victoria Station.

I'd been experienced in working with Hindus, whereas

Janette worked amongst the Muslim community. Now her furlough was nearly over the Mission was sending her back—not this time to India, but to a new work in Iran.

'Look, do you mind if I leave the two of you for a bit? I need to do some shopping. Our son needs a new jacket. And I might wander around Selfridges...' Helen asked, explaining she'd return in about an hour or so, which really meant two or three hours, at least.

Janette and I ordered another pot of tea.

'I'm fed up. I desperately want to be back in India. A short furlough is OK, but I want to be overseas. I don't belong here anymore—India's my home now. What am I to do, Janette?'

'Well, you can't storm the Indian Embassy. If you can't get a visa you'll need to come to terms with the fact that God is closing the door to you. I think you'll have to forget going to India and make a life for yourself in England. There's a great need here, too!'

I didn't intend to forget India. I reapplied several more times for a visa. The Mission did their best, too. It was hopeless. Eventually, I realised Janette was right—the door to India had closed to me.

What of the work out there? Who would take over the leprosy work? The Mission's representative in London reminded me that the work was the Lord's, not mine.

I resigned from the Mission, determined to get away from it all, to go to some place where no-one knew me. My faith had been shaken and I was so weary that I was prepared to give up the spiritual struggle. It seemed as if God had let me down.

In my loneliness and weariness I didn't possess the insight into what was happening—not an uncommon experience. John the Baptist, that child of the desert, after a whirlwind of hectic activity for the Kingdom of God, was imprisoned in the castle of Machaerus. In the solitude of his experience, depression and misunderstanding set in, and John asks, 'Are you the one who was to come, or should we expect someone else?' (Matthew 11:3). To this question, Jesus gives the answer: 'Blessed is the man who does not fall away on account of me' (Matthew 11:6).

How much I could have learnt from Elijah, Israel's greatest prophet. In his confrontation with Ahab and Jezebel, Elijah's splendid, intense nature gave way under the strain. Weariness and fear were expressed in his words, 'I am the only one left, and now they are trying to kill me too' (1 Kings 19:14). How graciously God dealt with his exhausted servant. He rested him, fed him and, afterwards, sent him on his way with a new task to perform.

The God of Elijah is still alive today and, unbeknown to me, he was providentially preparing my future.

The next few weeks were spent job hunting, and eventually a door opened in the north of England. Rotherham Corporation in conjunction with Sheffield University, were advertising in the *Nursing Times* for a Health Visitor-cum-field worker. I applied, was short listed and offered the post.

FOR REFLECTION

Jonah ran away from the Lord and headed for Tarshish (Jonah 1:3)

CHAPTER TWENTY ONE

Restoration and Renewal

I no longer felt exactly conscious of any divine purpose at work. In fact, I felt rather depressed with everything, as if God had forgotten me as I'd left behind both India and the familiarity of London. It was nevertheless, in a mood of grim determination, that I arrived in the North of England on what I saw as a tortuous path.

The north-bound train in which I found myself, without any warning began to make a grinding noise, and the next moment it gave a kind of lurching jump and came to a stop. A dispute seemed to be breaking out between the driver and a tall, fat man clad in an official British Rail uniform, both either stamping their feet or aggressively waving their arms in the air. Their words flowed past me. In an uncomprehending daze, I jumped down onto the platform and approached a porter who appeared ready to join in the terms of abuse.

'Excuse me,' I said, pulling my coat tighter around me, my breath coming in a long frosty stream. 'I need to get to Rotherham.'

'Ooh aye.'

'Well, are we far from there?'

He shook his head.

'Then if we are not far, would you tell me if it is within walking distance, please?'

'Depends.'

'On what?'

'On 'ow fit th'art. Th'sees, th'art in Doncaster reet nah!'

I raised my eyes and sighed. I left the station in search of a taxi to take me to my destination, for it was obvious that neither the train nor its driver was going any further.

'Will you please take me to Rotherham?' I asked.

'It'll cost yer, Miss.'

Cold and exasperated, I asked him if I looked as if I couldn't afford a taxi.

We were mostly silent on the way to my destination, but then the driver began to chuckle. 'What are thee goin't' Roth'room fer?'

'I have a job lined up. Tell me, what's so funny?'

His smile broke into full-blown laughter. 'Eee, I wor just thinkin' th'art too posh fer the larks of them in Roth'room!'

Arriving in the middle of January, the snow was laying deeply on the ground. The taxi driver decided, because of the weather, to go no further. He told me to catch a corporation bus. The biting wind was what was known as a lazy wind—it went straight through me instead of going around! I shivered and pulled up the fur-trimmed hood of my coat.

'Eee, lass, th'doest look snug under that 'at!', exclaimed an elderly man standing behind me in the queue.

Truly I had arrived in the North of England, as alien to me as India had once felt.

Starting my new post, I was well able to afford the rent on a spacious flat in a smart suburb of this industrial town. Materially, I was reasonably well off. Spiritually, I was a pauper.

For about eighteen months my life was surrounded by a non-Christian group of friends, both male and female. Then Beryl, one of my closest chums, a health visitor, gained promotion, which meant she had to move away.

Due to her absence, my social life took a rapid nosedive and I began to feel lonely. It was then I met Rory and began an unhelpful relationship, which ended in tears. I remember returning without him and making myself a meal now for one, and sitting down in front of the television. With nothing to interest me, I switched it off. My large, comfortable living room seemed to take on an uneasy silence. Now I felt isolated, unwanted and unloved.

A married couple, much older than I, did call in a couple of times a week, yet the sad and widespread malady of loneliness is not dispelled with a little chat now and again. The newspaper, the book, the little walk, the visit to the shops—how unsatisfying they were, how futile.

God had allowed me to follow my self appointed lifestyle long enough for me to realise that being offended either with him or his people, or both, carries no happy future.

One Sunday evening I turned on the radio and listened to the hymn singing. My room was filled with the haunting words of William Cowper's hymn:

"Where is the blessedness I knew
When first I saw the Lord?"

I knew now that I needed God as never before, but what to do for he seemed so far away?

That's it, I thought. I'm going to rectify this situation. I picked up the *Yellow Pages* and looked under 'Churches'. There was a telephone number listed of a Baptist Church. I made up my mind to dial but not on a Sunday evening when the minister would be tired, so I decided to wait until the next morning. Yet not on a Monday, for that might be his day off. Perhaps the day after... It took me at least two or three weeks before I telephoned him.

'I hope you don't mind my contacting you. I know how busy you must be, yet I really need some help,' I nervously blurted out.

'That's OK. We ministers only work on a Sunday, you know,' he joked. 'Now what can I do for you?'

Two hours later, I found myself sitting in his study. It was a dim, shabby room in need of decoration; the furniture had seen better days too. His books were not just on the shelves, but in untidy piles on the floor, on chairs, all over the place. His desk was equally untidy. How ever did he find anything when he worked in such chaos?

He sat back in his big old armchair, waiting for me to speak.

I blurted out my story, telling him how sad I was because I would never see India again. I confessed God to be no longer a part of my life. I told him everything.

He was thoughtful, frowning for a few moments. 'Well,' he analysed, 'the problem is that many Christians put ministers, and missionaries in particular, on a pedestal. They forget to toil in prayer for Christian workers in the front line of battle—and, oh boy, it is a battle too! Anyway, we mustn't blame our prayer partners too much, must we? What you've experienced has been close to a bereavement. What you need now is to rest in God's presence. He loves you, really he does.'

'I was taught that I should read my Bible and pray without ceasing, but I can't,' I wailed.

'Yep, sounds like pretty good advice, but for the time being, why not let me do the praying?'

As he prayed, the Lord's presence filled the room like a sweet smelling perfume and I experienced joy unspeakable and full of glory.

MEDITATION

There's a way back to God from the dark paths of sin;
There's a door that is open and you may go in;
At Calvary's Cross is where you begin,
    When you come as a sinner to Jesus.

CHAPTER TWENTY TWO

His Healing Power

"Jesus healed many who had various diseases."
(Mark 1:34)

SITTING in the optician's waiting room, I began to wonder what sort of spectacles would suit me best, when the adjoining door opened and I was called in to see him.

After chatting a while about nothing in particular, he began his examination by peering into my eyes with his opthalmascope.

Then the conversation took an unexpected turn.

'How long have you been a diabetic?' asked the optician.

'I'm not a diabetic,' I replied with a grin.

'You surely must be because you have a degree of retinopathy.'

I was not surprised at what the examination revealed, but for some strange reason I did not tell him that my 'tell tale eyes' were now a testimony to divine healing rather than Diabetes Mellitus.

My mind flashed back to April 1979 when, at the age of thirty-two years, I began to lose weight. I also consumed gallons of tea, coffee, or water in an attempt to quench the thirst that kept returning.

I arranged an evening appointment to see my medical practitioner in his surgery.

'You can go in now,' said the receptionist,' pointing the way, 'It's the first door on the left.'

I felt a little nervous as I entered his consulting room.

'Sit down, m'dear, and tell me what's wrong,' he said, glancing at my medical records.

'I've lost 2 stones in weight over the last two months. I am so tired and I cannot quench my thirst,'

He did a quick medical test, which showed a vastly abnormal amount of sugar and ketones in my blood.

'Well now, it's obvious what's wrong with you, isn't it?', he said, for he knew that I was medically trained.

'You're going to tell me that I am a diabetic, aren't you?'

I am so very sorry, Janice, really I am,' continued the doctor, 'I will arrange for you to see a senior physician at the General Hospital.'

I came out of the surgery and sat in the passenger seat of a friend's car. The friend, who was waiting outside the surgery, quizzed me as to what was wrong.

'Please, just take me home. I need to be alone,' I said, feeling as if I had just been given a life sentence. 'I need to get my thoughts in order.'

The following Tuesday came and I went to see the senior physician at the local General Hospital. The blood tests confirmed that I really did have Diabetes Mellitus. He prescribed 12 units of Actrapid Insulin and 24 units of Monotard Insulin to be given by daily injection. He also insisted on my having a 160 gram carbohydrate controlled diet.

'There's no reason why you cannot live a perfectly normal life, you know,' the physician said, obviously trying to reassure me.

'I hope so, but I cannot see my life in the future ever being the same again, can you?'

A perfectly normal life was something I certainly did not have. I became a 'brittle' diabetic, which meant that there was the likelihood of reacting to the insulin, or going into an insulin coma very quickly. On several occasions I woke up in a hospital ward and once I nearly died. I carried chocolate and glucose tablets in my handbag, but could not always do anything to help myself because of the confusion that accompanied the onset of an insulin reaction.

One day, while crossing a busy main road on my way home, it occurred to me that, if I did not have something to eat quickly, I might be in trouble. Reaching the island in the middle of the road, I stood and fumbled in my pocket for a sweet, but there was nothing there. I was beginning to feel distinctly queasy. I opened my handbag for some chocolate but it had been eaten the previous day and the supply had not been replaced. I looked in another compartment of my bag for a glucose tablet, but found the last remaining one in an inedible powdered form. I was becoming confused. I needed something to eat—*and quickly.* I tried to cross the road but I was too confused to reach the other side. I stepped out. Cars hooted and some drivers yelled at me. I staggered back to the island.

Two policemen saw me as I dropped to my knees on the island, my hands in the dirty wet gutter. They tried to pick me up and thinking I was drunk, bundled me into the back of their car and took me back to the Police Station.

What a smell! I looked around. Where was I? There was a bed standing in half of the small room. Upon the bed was an old, worn, grey and navy blue blanket and a striped, stained pillow without a pillow case. In the corner was a metal bucket! There were bars at the window and the strong sunlight shone through. The door was wide open and a tall, middle-aged man stood in the entrance.

'What on earth? Am I in a prison cell?' I asked, my voice gradually becoming louder. 'What have I done?'

'Are you feeling better, then?' enquired the man.

'Who are you? And why am I here?' I yelled.

'I am the Police Surgeon. Fortunately for you, the Desk Sergeant was an observant man and he noticed that, instead of sobering up, you were getting worse. It so happens that his daughter is a diabetic and something must have clicked in his mind. Quickly, he searched through your handbag and, finding your diabetic card he called me. I gave you an injection to bring up your blood sugar. You must now have a big drink of milk and then we'll arrange for you to have a high carbohydrate meal. Okay?'

'Okay,' I replied 'But I want to get out of this horrid, stinking cell. It is really bad. Ugh!'

The Surgeon laughed and called for a young constable, who was very kind and rustled me up a three-course meal in the Police canteen. I began to feel so much better.

Although the Police apologised for putting me 'inside', the incident was not without its humorous side. Together we laughed about the teetotaller that was committed to a cell for drunkenness!

Occasionally I attended a Pentecostal assembly when the weather conditions prevented me from driving across the town to the Baptist Church. At the Pentecostal Church I grew accustomed to the way that sick people were invited to come forward for healing. The pastor and elders would lay hands on the sick and sometimes wonderfully miraculous things happened. But not always. It was not an uncommon sight to see disappointed people taking their infirmities and sicknesses back home again.

What I did not like there was the way the unhealed were blamed for not having enough faith to be healed. It was pathetic to see some sick people trying desperately to obtain more faith, or analysing their faith, in a hopeless effort to discover its deficiency, and thinking this was keeping them from the healing power of God.

There is, I feel, a real mystery about divine healing. Paul said that he left Trophimus at Miletus sick and he prayed to the Lord three times for his own healing, but received his answer in the words, "My grace is sufficient for you." (2 Corinthians 12:9) To blame a sufferer for lack of faith is both cruel and unkind and it is not an answer that satisfies me.

However, God is good and does not refuse to work because the emphasis is not quite right. On about six occasions I too went forward to receive the laying on of hands without anything happening whatsoever. Then, in the November of 1979, the conviction was borne in upon me that I was only wanting healing to get rid of the inconvenience of being a diabetic. I felt that healing would only take place when I wanted it all for the glory of God.

One Sunday evening, as the service drew to a close, the invitation from the letter of James was given: 'Is any sick among you; let him call for the elders of the church and let them pray over him, anointing him with oil in the name of the Lord: And the prayer of faith shall save the sick' (James 5:14-15, AV). I went forward and the pastor and elders laid hands on my head and prayed for me.

My healing took place there and then, but I did not know it. There were no feelings or any indication that anything had happened. Next morning I gave myself an insulin injection as usual and quickly went into a coma. I was admitted to the General Hospital as an emergency.

'Why on earth did you give yourself insulin? I was asked. 'A healthy person cannot tolerate insulin.'

When I saw the physician and told him what happened, he performed a 'glucose tolerance test' upon me which was normal. He confirmed that I was no longer a diabetic! He was at a loss to understand it with his medical mind, but could not deny the reality of the healing. He wrote to my general practitioner that they had witnessed a miracle

Standing up to testify to God's power to heal was something of a thrill. There was only one thing that cast a shadow over the occasion and that was the face of a doctor friend. He was a diabetic and a man of faith who was not healed. How I wished that he stood with me, saying the same happy things that I was able to say, but it was, for some inexplicable reason, not to be.

Medical records uphold the facts concerning my diabetes and my subsequent healing.

A CHALLENGE

I am no longer my own, but yours. Put me to what you will, rank me with whom you will; put me to doing, put me to suffering; let me be employed for you or laid aside for you, exalted for you or brought low for you; let me be full, let me be empty; let me have all things, let me have nothing; I freely and wholeheartedly yield all things to your pleasure and disposal. And now, glorious and blessed God, Father, Son, and Holy Spirit, you are mine and I am yours. So be it. And the covenant now made on earth, let it be ratified in heaven. Amen.

(Taken from the Methodist Covenant Service)

CHAPTER TWENTY-THREE

The Wardress

I CREPT into the morning service and sat in my usual seat. (Janet, a friend, who nearly always sat with me was away on a course.) It had become the norm in that little chapel for everyone to congregate ten minutes before the services began in an attempt to dissuade the usual stragglers from being late. To prevent the regular pre-service chatter, we would all join in the singing of choruses. 'He lives' seemed to be a particular favourite at the time and the volume went up. We were just singing it through for a second time when a visitor came and, seeing the empty chair next to me, asked in a whisper if that was anyone's seat. I shook my head.

Just over an hour or so later, as the service was brought to a close, the pastor stood by the door shaking hands with the congregation as they filed out. This visiting pastor, not an over popular chap, was in the habit of droning on, completely oblivious of the time, and at the end of the service he stood by the door, shaking hands and chatting with everyone at length, fully aware that the women were anxious to get home and rescue their roasts!

Nevertheless, I held back even longer to greet the visitor, a woman old enough to be around my parents' age. She was a thin person with a tired looking appearance; her eyes lacked lustre and her skin hung in empty folds around her neck. 'It is good to see you here. Have you come from far?' I asked.

She explained that she lived alone, and so on. As we chatted I couldn't help noticing her heavy guttural accent, too strong for Scandinavian or Dutch. It had to be something like German.

'Where do you hail from originally?' I enquired. 'Your English is very good.'

'Oh, I come from Germany, but I've been here quite a while.'

'Really? So what made you come to England? You must miss Germany, for it's a beautiful country.'

'Sure. I once loved Germany, but I got out quickly after the war; just between you and me, I didn't want to be accused of doing anything against the Jews...' she started.

I cocked my head to one side, curious to know more of what she meant.

'People like me were only obeying orders. I didn't want to do what I did, but I might have been shot otherwise.'

I glowered at her. 'If you are saying what I think you are, I'd better tell you that I am Jewish.'

'Jewish? You are Jewish and yet you are here in this church instead of being in a synagogue? Why? Isn't it tantamount to heresy?'

'No. I am a Jewess but I found the Lord as my Saviour back in 1962. I am now a Christian, yet being such doesn't mean that I am no more Jewish.'

'No. I do not understand.'

'Well, let me explain. When someone like me believes in Jesus as our Messiah we return to the God of Abraham, Isaac and Jacob, fulfilled and completed. Do you see what I mean now?'

She frowned and lowered her eyes, ignoring my explanation. 'Have you heard of Auschwitz?'

'Who hasn't? It was in there that my dad nearly died.'

Now her sad eyes stared up at me as I explained how

he was captured at the battle of El Alamein and thrown into a prisoner of war camp. When he was found to be Jewish he was transferred to Auschwitz.

'Oh dear, how can I ever begin to tell you... you will probably hate me and there is no time now to explain my story in full. It's just that I was employed as a wardress in the women's section there. I was the one who used to instruct the women—mostly Jews, of course—to strip and go into the showers.'

'But they weren't showers, were they?'

'That's right,' she said. 'If the women had any children I instructed them to clutch them very close and to breath deeply. It was I who, under instructions, led thousands of Jews to their deaths. I was probably one of the most cruel of all the wardresses. Yet, here we are in this church together—me an ex-wardress of Auschwitz and you a Jewess... both now Christians, eh? I know that God has forgiven me for what I did...'

I felt like I was a volcano ready to erupt. 'I am sorry, but you must excuse me. I must go home.'

The pastor was still chatting at the door but, mindlessly, I almost ignored his outstretched hand and made for my car where I sat, staring into nothing maybe for a quarter of an hour. Finally, starting up the engine, I drove off. On the way home I saw the woman waiting at a bus stop. She attempted to flag me down, but I made out I hadn't seen her.

Still shocked at what she'd told me, I didn't feel I could give her a lift. How could she just have sat there and told me, of all people, how she was personally responsible for the deaths of thousands of Jews? I would rather have been shot than do what she did. She'd made my people walk to their deaths. 'No, Fraulein,' I muttered as I passed her by. 'You can walk, not to your death, but to your flat, free of filthy water, rats, leeches and the smell of death and decay.' I was born in 1946 and precisely one year before that she was killing Jews.

Then my conscience got at me. Reaching the next roundabout, I decided to go back to the bus stop where she'd been waiting. I'd give her a lift, but I would not get involved in any pleasantries, not with her, yet I could at least drive her home. To leave an elderly woman stranded in the cold for a couple of hours would be inhumane on my part, although I hadn't considered my behaviour towards her to already have been inhumane.

I arrived back at the bus stop, but she was gone. Having a rough idea where she lived, I began to drive slowly along in that direction, but I couldn't find her.

Gosh, why am I bothering about her? I thought with annoyance. She didn't bother about what happened to all those Jewish women and children whom she sent to the gas chambers. She only cared for her own skin. And how could she say she was now a Christian?

The Holy Spirit, it must have been him, brought to my mind part of the chorus which we'd been singing at the start of the morning service: 'He walks with me and He talks with me—' But he wasn't, not then, for I wasn't allowing him in to talk with me regarding that wardress. I'd closed my mind and taken on board the haughty attitude that she should not have dared to speak to me, of all people, as if I were, for some reason, superior because I was a Messianic Jewess, one of God's elect.

'He lives within my heart.' Really? Someone was living in my heart but the Lord wasn't being allowed much living space.

'I grieve at your separation, my child,' He said. 'Come unto me.'

At six-twenty p.m I was once again in my usual seat, ready for the usual start of the evening service. I glanced at the empty seat by my side. Oblivious to the chorus singing, I wondered if the German woman would be there. What a daft thought! After the despicable way I'd behaved that morning she was unlikely to ever come again—not to our chapel.

'If ye do not forgive men their trespasses,' Jesus said, 'neither will your Father forgive your trespasses' (Matthew 6:14,15, AV). I lowered my eyes and asked the Lord to forgive me, telling him that I was sorry. What had happened was a shattering experience, but I'd learned that in my own strength I was incapable of love. The power to love came to me from the Holy Spirit, 'because God's love has been poured into our hearts through the Holy Spirit which has been given to us.' (Romans 5:5, RSV).

I prayed that I would be able to meet the Fraulein again, to ask for her forgiveness, but I never saw her again.

MEDITATION

Should I give up trying because I fail?

CHAPTER TWENTY-FOUR

The Empire Strikes Back

(1977)

THERE was a soft thud as the Boeing's wheels hit the tarmac, followed by a shrill scream of brakes as the powerful jet decelerated down the runway at Manchester Airport.

The short flight from Holland where I'd been holidaying had been smooth and uneventful. Jennifer, a friend who'd been staying at my flat, would be waiting to meet me.

The engines wound down to a muted whine as the plane wheeled off the runway, then cruised towards its allotted bay.

Customary procedures completed, I joined the queue of passengers to the lounge.

'Janice.'

I summoned a smile in greeting.

Within only a short time we were in her maroon-coloured Escort, parked at the kerbside immediately adjacent to the entrance, ready to exit the terminal.

Jennifer cast me a glance. 'You look as if your holiday's done you good…' she trailed off. 'You've quite a lot of mail waiting for you. I've left it for you in your study, on your desk. Some's obviously junk mail but one looks very official.'

Back in my flat, I began to sort through my mail. There,

at first, seemed nothing of consequence—a few bills, a postcard from a girl friend on a Swiss vacation and a letter from the Prime Minister's secretary, a letter of importance. As I began to open it, I cast the others aside to be dealt with another time.

Flopping down on the sofa, I propped my feet on the coffee table and focused carefully on the contents.

'Anything wrong?' Jennifer asked. 'You've a strange expression on your face.'

I gaped at her. 'You'll never guess what—I'm being considered for an OBE.'

She crossed the floor in three strides and plonked down on the sofa beside me. 'A what?'

'That's right—an OBE.'

Oh, Janice, how marvellous! When will you get it?'

'I'm only being considered—it seems it's something to do with my work with lepers.'

The letter was so unexpected, it knocked me for six. And I was not entirely sure it was right; there were so many who'd worked longer and harder than I who surely merited not just an OBE, but a knighthood.

All of my senses alert, it was difficult to empty my head of every thought. The night seemed endless and sleep eluded me until a chink of light was beaming through a gap in my curtains; it was morning.

So as not to wake my guest, still apparently fast asleep in the next bedroom, I crept my way along to the bathroom where I splashed cold water on my face, patted it dry with a towel and began to clean my teeth.

After brushing my hair and anchoring the mass of unruly curls into a ponytail, I swung away from the mirror and dressed rapidly in a loose, beige cotton skirt and a blue sloppy sweater. Slipping my feet into soft brown leather loafers, I wandered off to double-check the contents of my letter.

A moment later the study door opened and Jennifer flashed a huge grin. 'Morning!' she exclaimed.

At only twenty-eight, my friend was, as she saw it, at the height of her profession, although other midwives were more senior. Jenny was content to be the senior ward sister at a maternity hospital in Glasgow. She was of medium height, slim and spry with rosy cheeks in a merry face, and a twinkle in her sea-blue eyes. She missed being someone's wife with a happy marriage and a couple of children, yet she could dream; maybe it still wasn't too late for either of us—God knew.

'I've been doing a lot of thinking throughout the night,' I began. 'If this OBE is actually offered... I don't think I'll accept it.'

'Why ever not?'

I shook my head. 'It'd all be wrong. I don't deserve it. If I'd spent a life-time with lepers I could understand it, but... oh, I dunno.'

'You must have done something good,' said Jenny, disbelievingly. 'In the time I've known you you've rarely told me much about your work. What did you do?'

'The main part of my work for the Mission was in the field of leprosy...'

To be or not to be, to do it or not to do it. My role, under the umbrella of the Mission in conjunction with the local Government was 'to be and to do it'—to get on with what was needed in the lives of those regarded as the most wretched of society. Delivering the babies of the lepers, district nursing through which I'd seek out those displaying the early signs of leprosy, research into the disease, the training of locals to care for the patients in a ward I'd set aside for lepers. It all sounded so mighty, but it was as nothing compared with what was going on, for example, in the Leprosy Mission, and other such societies.

If I could have been left completely to my own devices

I would have spent almost all my waking hours rescuing the young twelve year old girls, many of them lepers, from being sold to the Hindu priests who kept them in the temples for either their own sexual pleasures or for the evils of prostitution.

I looked up at my friend. 'If such practices outraged me, what did it do to the heart of the Lord? I cannot comprehend. Maybe any OBE should be a sort of tribute to the kids; or perhaps my tribute should be telling the world about them and their plight, whatever it takes.'

I sat, remembering those days when I went off on my own on the hazardous journey across to Pune, schooling myself to resist the temptation to bite the local Governor's head off concerning those temple girls. He never welcomed my regular visits; there was a courage, a fearlessness when I approached him and he didn't like it. I wanted something done, but he claimed it was all of little consequence, a far-fetched idea, therefore it was all too easy to try and dismiss me… or so he thought!

One day he looked crushed at my visit, then instantly his face brightened and he said, 'Tell you what, why don't you go back to England and fall in love? Don't wag your finger at me, Miss Finger Wagger! You're not wearing a ring, so I know you are not married. There's obviously no special man in your life—if there were you wouldn't have the time to bother about those urchins. How does that sound?'

'What sort of fool do you think I am? Every time I come to see you, you try to fob me off. I'm not moving until you give me a Government official, or two, to get those kids out of the temples.'

My regular visits continued until one day the Governor had had enough and I was taken by surprise. I was given two officials, one woman and one man; the three of us thumbed our noses at the danger and took from the temple about thirty sad little kids.

I sang songs of praise as I took them to Ooty where the Mission ran a school, mainly for orphaned girls.

However, I was soon back to see the Governor whose heart sank at my presence. 'Take your time, Sahib,' I said. I'm going nowhere. Not until you help me to release more children from other temples.' He sat gazing down, his elbows on his knees, his head propped in his hands, his face settling into morose lines, for he knew to refuse me would mean more visits.

My work had prospered but not in my own strength. The work was the Lords.

Jennifer cut in. 'Who would you have to accompany you? That is, if you do go to London to get your OBE?'

'Are you offering?' I grinned.

Jenny shook her head, explaining Glasgow was a bit too far for a day or two in London. 'But you know who'd be in her element, don't you?' she grinned.

There was no question in our minds—Helen! we laughed.

As it turned out, I was officially offered the OBE and my old friend Helen, who really should have been born the daughter of an earl with the honorary title of a Lady, would accompany me. Instead she was the third child of an out of work musician who lived in a dilapidated flat. Determined to free herself from her upbringing, she married well, to a barrister with a double-barrelled name; this suited her well.

The thought of accompanying me to Buckingham Palace appealed to her so much that one would have thought it was she who was getting a gong.

Helen lugged me to the most fashionable shops she knew in the West End of London, not forgetting Harrods, of course. In one store, I can't remember which, a sales assistant glided over towards me and, before I could withdraw, enquired, 'What exactly Madam was looking for?'

Giving her a chilly smile, I was struck dumb, unlike Helen who propelled me to the rails. 'She's going to Buck House—we both are—O.B.E. you know,' as if she had a plum in her mouth.

Several hours later we emerged with what no woman of fashion could be without!

Next I was bustled off to the shoe shop—not one shop, but almost all of them. Returning to the first shop again, we were directed to muted and elegant court shoes; something we could stand in all day and that looked rather nice.

All I wanted was to sit in a café and have a cup of coffee and something wickedly fattening to eat, but Helen hadn't finished. There was the hat.

'Hats don't sit well over my curly hair,' I protested.

'You wear one to church, don't you? Well then, come on, we need a hat each. Wide brims might be the best.'

'All this is wearing me out. I should never have consented to this OBE; after all, what use is it? And all this shopping—I hate shopping.'

Helen gaped at me, shocked by my remarks concerning the OBE. 'What use is it? What use is it? How could you say such a thing? I can't believe what I' m hearing!

There was a sense of pleasurable anticipation for the day ahead when, in our new togs, the two of us ordered a taxi to take us to Buckingham Palace, having spent a night in a local hotel.

A Palace official instructed me, along with others receiving awards, as to what we were supposed to do when we were confronted by Her Majesty, how to answer her questions, and how to know when she'd had enough of listening to us.

All too soon it was my turn. Now, did the official say I had to call her Ma'am to rhyme with jam, or Ma'am to rhyme with arm? Oh dear, I just could not remember; what if I said the wrong thing? I'd carry the mistakes to my grave.

Suddenly she was before me and my stomach muscles stiffened. She was shorter than I imagined, no more than 5'3". Wafting in exotic perfume, her red designer outfit was a stunning compliment to her ageing, but good looks. Her features were a carefully composed mask, and my eyes held hers for a few timeless seconds as she asked me... oh, dear, what was it now?... about my leprosy work, how long I'd worked in India.

Dear me, I can't remember what I'd said, but it was all over in a brief milli-second, which was unlike me for I have been accused of never using one word when two or three would do.

Outside the Palace I had my photograph taken holding out my medal. Not to be outdone, Helen organised herself, her memorable day at the Palace, her day with that hat.

All that shopping, all those sore, aching feet and our ginormous hats had culminated in a piece of metal in a box, to spend its days in the back of the drawer of a sideboard.

MEDITATION

Just what have I really done for the Lord? Is there much more that I could do?

Give me the lowest place: or if for me
    That lowest place too high, make one more low
Where I may sit and see
    My God and love Thee so

(Christina Rossetti)

CHAPTER TWENTY-FIVE

Two Are Better Than One

IT was 'Last of the Summer Wine' country, the home of Nora Batty with her wrinkled stockings, so I had been told.

From the very moment, back in 1981, when I first arrived in Holmfirth, I had been entranced by the beauty of the surrounding countryside. Whatever the mood of the weather, a day rarely passed without catching my breath in surprise and delight at one thing or another. In an infinite number of small and grand ways, nature, in all its glory, was constantly revealing itself to me in this corner of West Yorkshire.

Turning left I strolled along to the little Methodist chapel, enjoying the walk after being cooped up in the hospital all day where I was employed as a ward sister.

And there he was again. I had seen him before and a faint smile touched my mouth. The man did not have glamorous movie-star looks, although he was quite good looking in a clean cut way. He had a nice face, that was the best way of describing it, and it was one that was open and honest. His slightly receding hair was dark, his eyes brown, their expression gentle and his mouth was quick to smile. He was about five feet nine in height. A pleasant, ordinary sort of chap, I decided, as he seated himself in the pew in front of where I was sitting. Spellbound, as I seemed to be, he was older than me, maybe old enough to be too old for me, although he appeared boyishly younger.

After the service I went across to shake hands with this stranger, but he'd turned away to speak with someone else.

In another part of the Methodist Circuit there was St David's Church—a shared Anglican-cum-Methodist Church with an evangelical vicar. Discovering that I'd been a missionary in India, he invited me to tell of my experiences—those busy fruitful days.

Although God had brought me home from India, I knew he still had other plans for me: 'For I know the plans I have for you, says the Lord, plans for welfare and not for evil, to give you a future and a hope.' (Jeremiah 29:11 RSV). As for my future, I didn't yet know who or what it involved. All I needed to do was trust my loving heavenly Father each step of the way.

Aware I was new to the area and having seen me in church, the Rev Gerald Barraclough, the Methodist Superintendent minister called in at my house to see me; a sort of pastoral visit, to introduce himself.

'Oh, um, by the way, I wonder if you know who the man was who was sitting in front of me last Sunday?' I asked, and promptly began to describe this stranger in such detail that Mr Barraclough, a twinkle in his eyes, gave me a knowing smile.

'Oh, I think that must be Mark. Sometimes he preaches here in the Holmfirth Circuit,' explained the minister. 'He works for the Head Post Office in Huddersfield as a Postal Officer. Right now he's living with his widowed mother.'

I grinned, raising my eyes to the heavens. 'At his age?'

'Now, don't be mistaken or get the wrong end of the stick... .Mark's no mummy's boy! It's just convenient, I suppose, for he's not married... never has been.'

He explained further that Mark had been in the regular army for eight years until 1951 when he was released to go to Cliff College—an evangelistic training centre in Derbyshire. 'His hobby's photography—in fact, he's passionate about it, yet not as passionate as he is concerning God.'

'Photography, eh? Hmm...'

My visitor nodded. 'Why, do you like photography, too?'

'Not yet,' I grinned.

That week I made a trip to Dixons in Huddersfield and purchased a new Olympus SLR camera.

The following Sunday I finally managed to come face to face with Mark 'I've been hearing how you're a keen photographer...'

'Yes, very much indeed. What about you?'

I informed him how only that very week I'd acquired a camera, but I didn't quite know how to work it, and maybe he could show me!

He agreed. 'I've a day off this Thursday and I'm planning on going by the train to Sheffield to photograph the cathedral. Perhaps you'd like to come along? It'd give you a chance to get the hang of your camera.'

Various outings followed, and we mutually decided to continue our friendship until one evening, just before we were about to go to our prospective homes, he stared at me, a peculiar expression on his face.

'What's wrong?' I asked.

'I love you, Janice, I really am in love with you.'

I gaped at him. 'What?'

'You heard what I said.' Mark, there and then, went down on one knee 'Will you marry me? Please, Janice, say you will.'

We celebrated our engagement at the Three Nuns, a restaurant in Mirfield. The candlelight threw a warm and rosy glow over the scene which seemed to be a reflection of our feelings—our romance, a romance for life.

From the moment we announced our engagement, life became a matter of decisions, an exciting whirl of plans and preparations. My dress, my shoes, a bridesmaid, the cake and the flowers. And then there was our first home to organise: colours, fabrics, patterns, plates and glass, table linen, pretty sheets for the bedroom, and carpets for the floor. What to choose? Where to start? There was so much to do.

Our wedding day eventually arrived. The beribboned white Rolls Royce drove me to the picturesque setting of a little Methodist Chapel situated on the outskirts of Dewsbury in West Yorkshire. The chauffeur followed a delightful route along country lanes, avoiding the industrial area in the valley below.

The torrential morning rain stopped and the sunshine began to break through the clouds, turning an unpromising start to the day into a glorious afternoon.

The official photographer was waiting. I don't like having my photograph taken, yet there was no escaping on this day; I very much wanted a photographic record for posterity. He was not the only one with a camera. Some of the locals congregated around the gates of the chapel with their little cameras—it seemed everyone wanted a photo and my face ached as I kept up a smile for the popping flashbulbs.

Groomed to almost perfection, I walked slowly down the short aisle. The minister, a tall man dressed in a long black cassock, belted at the waist, peered over his glasses and smiled, trying to put me at ease, for under the froth of pink and white tulle my knees knocked!

The man about to become my husband stood on my right. There were no doubts—he was God's choice for me. He loved me and I loved him.

Suddenly, I collected my thoughts as the minister proclaimed, 'We are gathered here in the presence of God to witness the marriage of Janice and Mark, to support them with our prayers and to share their joy. Marriage is given by God. It is not to be entered upon or thought of lightly or selfishly; but responsibly and in the love of God... Such marriage is the foundation of true family life and, when blessed with the gift of children...

Children? At our age? I was thirty-seven, Mark, twenty years my senior. I didn't think so.

MEDITATION

For this reason a man will leave his father and mother and be united with his wife, and the two will become one flesh (Matthew 19:5).

Have we learned to really trust the One who made us 'male and female'?

Are we determined to seek the best in our marriage?

How can we really demonstrate to the world the beauty of Christian marriage?

CHAPTER TWENTY-SIX

The Unexpected

TO be perfectly honest, almost everything in my life has been unexpected and the thoughts that were buzzing around in my head following the wedding ceremony were truly unexpected. The minister who conducted the service read from the service book, 'Such marriage is the foundation of the true family and when blessed with children...'

Blessed with children?

When I was in my early twenties I longed for a baby so much that sometimes I could hardly bear the frustration of being childless.

Now I was thirty-seven, Mark fifty-seven. I tried to imagine what it would be like to have a child—to live with it day by day and, worst of all, night by night!

Mark and I openly discussed most things together prior to our marriage, but the matter of having a child never came into our conversations, so I needed to find the right moment to bring up this subject.

'Oh, but, Mark, don't you think having a baby would be absolutely lovely?—ooh, Mark, just think our very own baby...' I began one evening.

'Yes, I am thinking, and I'm thinking straight—about the realities, which are a bit more complicated. It would be with us twenty-four hours a day, seven days a week... and what about our jobs? Are you prepared to abandon a career? And then there's our church life, our social life,' replied Mark, shaking his head. 'And what is more, aren't we a bit old to start a family. Neither of us are in the first flush of youth, me especially. I might be dead before the child is a teenager.'

'I still think it would be wonderful to bring a little one into the world.' I stated.

Mark remained unconvinced.

I went to see our general practitioner about another minor matter and asked him if it would be wise for me at my age to have a baby—after all, my age was regarded as the life expectancy in 1850.

'I'm thirty-seven. Is it crazy to think about getting pregnant at my age? I could have a less than perfect baby, couldn't I?'

'You have been a midwife and health visitor and you know that the answer is 'Yes' to both your questions, but it is obvious you are determined to have a baby and listening to reason won't stop you. But be assured, if you do get pregnant you know you will have the very best of obstetric care. OK?'

Al I needed was to convince Mark.

Four month's later I felt very dizzy and began to be sick. I craved either porridge or salad-cream sandwiches. I couldn't face tea or coffee, only pineapple juice or cold cocoa! The doctor hardly needed to confirm that I was pregnant, and together Mark and I began to look forward to the time when we would welcome into our home our little baby.

The pregnancy seemed to us like a major miracle. The first time I felt the baby move inside me, something of primal importance happened in my inner-most self. I, with all women, with all time, felt utterly and irrevocably female.

I remember many feelings. Some confused, some startling. I had a strange feeling of invasion. Another living being was temporarily inhabiting my body and I loved it.

Yet I was frightened of what was happening, and of the unknown. Was it possible to be this nauseated and still live? I was also apprehensive about my time in labour and the pain that would accompany it. I was fearful in case my baby was abnormal. All this turmoil was going on, of course, at the same time as I was growing smugly proud of myself for being pregnant. To me it was as amazing as life on another planet.

However, the pregnancy did not progress as easily as I hoped and I needed to spend sixteen long weeks in bed. Because of my age and the problems that were arising throughout the pregnancy I always saw a senior obstetrician.

She was an unattractive woman. In fact, the first time I saw her I thought she was a man until I noticed her skirt! She shouted at almost everyone, especially the Pakistani men who brought their wives to the ante-natal clinic. The Pakistani men would occupy the seats in the waiting room whilst their tired, pregnant wives would stand up. This would so enrage the obstetrician that she would shout at these men and make them wait outside. Her language at the time was invariably very bad, but she called it 'colourful'.

Most of the midwifery staff and the junior doctors who worked at the clinic were apparently as unnerved by this female as I was. One member of the staff would 'keep an eye out' for the arrival of the obstetrician. When her car pulled into its own private parking space, all the staff would take up their positions. She would then march in, not stopping for anything or anyone that was in her way, and the work would begin in earnest.

Towards the end of my pregnancy, I was breathlessly lying flat on my back on a couch in a cubicle of the ante-natal clinic waiting for the obstetrician to come.

She duly arrived and began to examine my bump.

'How old are you? Thirty-EIGHT! You must be mad!' she said, still pushing my 'bump' around. 'Why have a first baby at your age?'

She told me that the baby was coming feet first and that she was unable to make it turn around to ensure that it would be head first. In her usual direct way, she told me that I would need a caesarean section due to the position of the baby. She obviously could not put the baby of a thirty eight year old woman at risk by allowing her to go into labour and deliver a 'breech'. So it made sense for me to have a caesarean section.

I went home with the obstetrician's words still ringing in my ears, 'There's not a obstetrician in the country who can turn that baby. It's a "fixed breech".'

Mark tried to comfort me, without success. I was not open to reason.

That evening we went to a prayer meeting at the Methodist Church where we were members. The Minister and his wife Anne were parents of two year old twins and we were able to share things with them. After the meeting we stayed behind for a coffee and I told them that I was to have a caesarean section because the baby was a breech

'Would you like Anne and me to pray?' the Minister asked me in his quiet voice.

I was surprised by the suggestion. After the obstetrician's authoritative pronouncement, it did not occur to Mark and me that it was a matter of prayer, for it was so final.

'If you want to,' I replied with a sigh. 'Why not?'

They prayed and, as they did, the baby seemed more active than ever. This also seemed to increase the heartburn and breathlessness from which I suffered during the latter part of the pregnancy.

The following week I, still with my bump, waddled along to yet another antenatal check up.

Once again I breathlessly climbed onto the couch and awaited the arrival of the obstetrician.

She marched into the cubicle and began to feel how the baby was lying.

'That's funny,' she said, 'most odd!'

'What is?' I asked.

She ignored my question and called for the senior midwife. Complete panic seemed to fill my whole being. Whatever was wrong? Why was she calling for the midwife? Why would she not answer my question when I asked what was wrong?

The midwife came and palpated my abdomen. She agreed that it was funny.

Why would they not tell me what was 'funny'?

'WHAT'S WRONG?' I asked in a louder tone. 'TELL ME, PLEASE!'

'Nothing, absolutely nothing!' came the reply from the obstetrician with a smile.

She told me that the baby had turned, although it was actually too big to do so. It was now coming head first instead of feet first and so I would not need a Caesarean Section. I would have a normal delivery unless, of course, anything went wrong in labour.

'I don't understand how that could have happened, though,' said the obstetrician, frowning and shaking her head.

I explained that the minister and his wife prayed with me about the position of baby.

I waited for the reactions from the obstetrician and the midwife.

'Well,' replied the obstetrician, 'I never believed in God, but no-one else could have turned that baby. There isn't an obstetrician in the country who could have turned that baby. It was too big to actually turn around by itself. It must have been your God.'

The obstetrician then turned to the Midwife and asked her if she believed in God.

The midwife shuffled her feet and looked embarrassed.

'Well?' bellowed the obstetrician, 'Do you?'

She suddenly remembered an urgent job that just could not wait and rushed away!

On the following Friday morning at 6 a.m. I began to have severe backache. Then the contractions started. I told Mark it was time to go to the hospital. He raced to get the car out of the garage. My small suitcase was thrown onto the back seat. Then he realised that it would be a good idea if he put me in the car, too!

The hospital was a long drive from where we lived and we seemed to catch every red traffic light along the way.

On arrival at the hospital, I was taken to my own room where I was examined. The contractions were coming thick and fast, but they were not causing the labour to progress. At 3 p.m. I was given medication to rectify things. It worked.

The midwife was suddenly assisting the delivery of our baby whilst Mark was still trying to tie up the back of her sterile green gown. At 3.25 p.m. a baby cried. We had a son! And it was a normal delivery. It was a happy day—one to treasure for ever, even though it seemed long and arduous for me. The midwife began to tell Mark to give me a kiss. She was too late. I was holding our new son in one arm and my other arm was round my husband's neck as he kissed me. He was so overcome by the whole emotional experience that I could feel his wet salty tears on my face.

We were now a family.

Matthew was perfect, weighing in at 8lb. 2oz. on 31st August, 1984.

FOR PRAYER AND MEDITATION

Oh, Lord, help us to glorify you in the power to love, both in our marriage and to our child(ren). Above all, may we pour out our love for you so that we can give a fragrance all around. In Jesus' name. Amen.

CHAPTER TWENTY SEVEN

God's Special Agent

JENNY, our little Cairn terrier, jumped up around my legs in a frenzied dance as I clipped the lead to her collar. 'You won't be able to demand a walk just when you want after the baby's born,' I explained, just as if she understood my every word. 'In future you'll have to be content to run around the garden until your master arrives home.'

We strolled through the estate, along by all the newly built houses. In the front garden of one dwelling a woman, probably in her late fifties, was tackling some patches of docks and an overgrowth of thistles. Holding her back and stretching she looked up and smiled at me. 'I just don't know where all these weeds come from!' she exclaimed, making polite conversation. 'I say, should you be trailing your little dog out in your condition, and on such a hot day?'

'Well, I did have other plans, like sitting with my feet up in the cool of our lounge, but I'm afraid I tend to spoil this young pup.'

'Listen, would you like to come indoors and join me in a cold drink . I have some home-made lemonade in the fridge.'

'Thank you. If you are really sure…'

'Absolutely. It'd be a great excuse to get out of the gardening.'

As we sat together she asked when my baby was due and was most surprised to discover it was to be our first child.

'I hope you won't think me impertinent, dear, but aren't

you taking an enormous risk having a baby at your age?' asked my newly acquired Job's comforter, readily listing the problems our little one might encounter such as Down's Syndrome, spina-bifida, and so on.

Finishing the drink, I politely made my excuses and left. That evening when Mark returned from work, he asked me how I was.

I shrugged. 'Oh, OK, I suppose.'

'You don't sound very sure.'

'Mark, you don't think there could be anything wrong with our baby, do you?'

'No, of course not. You've had scans and that... um... what do you call that other test? That amnio thing was all right, wasn't it?'

'Amniocentesis,' I corrected.

'Yes, that. That showed everything was just fine, so why on earth are you worrying?'

I told Mark all about my encounter with Maureen. 'She knew of other women whose tests were normal and yet she said they had abnormal babies. Just supposing our one was not quite perfect... oh, how would we cope? And what about my friend Helen? She lost her baby only minutes after giving birth.'

'And you should know better, Janice, for you've been a midwife both here and in India. You, of all people, should have more sense than to listen to a neighbour. Frankly, I think it would be best if you kept well away from her in the future, especially if she's going to upset you with her tales of doom and gloom.'

When Matthew was born at 3.25 pm. on the 31st August, 1984 at the Bradford Royal Infirmary, he was just perfect, weighing in at 81b. 2oz. To us, as doting parents, he was the most beautiful child born to mankind. My fears were needless.

One evening, not long after being discharged from the

hospital, I was busying myself upstairs in the nursery, tucking Matthew down in his cradle. As I smiled down at our baby, my mind travelled back in time to the late rabbi, Sir John Flowers. How thrilled he would have been to have seen his great grandson, the child of his favourite grand-daughter, to have watched him grow, to have sat him on his knee in front of the crackling of his coal fire and tell him of his days at Magdalen College, where the bells of Oxford echo throughout the city. Oh, how the old man would have hoped upon hope that Matthew would enter that world to become an academic with a mind like a sword, along with the beauty of goodness. As for me, I naturally wanted the best for him with his early years to be peaceful and secure, safe and happy in our home.

'Janice, Maureen is here. May she pop up and see the baby?' Mark called up the stairs, bringing me back to the reality of the moment.

'Is it convenient?'

She came up and peered into the cradle at the sleeping bundle. 'Oh, Janice, he's just adorable, isn't he? Nevertheless, you'll have to keep a close eye on him.'

I looked quizzical. 'What do you mean? Why…?'

'M'dear, you must have read about the recent number of cot deaths that have been reported in the local press,' Maureen carried on. 'Why, even only last month a couple in the next street from me found their baby dead in the pram… and the mother was a doctor as well!'

She worried and frustrated me. I knew her words should have fallen on deaf ears, but I hardly slept for the anxiety. I used to creep in and check on Matthew to see if he was still breathing. I pleaded with the Lord, night after night, that he would not take our only child. I nearly choked on the 'Thy will be done' bit.

After six long weeks of pleadings, I was tucking him

down when I looked up; there, standing behind and over the cot was a very tall, white being with wings outstretched, whose brilliance I could not measure. Then he, or it, disappeared. Stunned and amazed, I knew I'd seen an angel—God's secret agent guarding our son.

Releasing all my pent up tensions, the Lord brought to mind a verse: 'My God has sent his angel, and hath shut the lions' mouth' (Daniel 6:22, AV)

I never heard from Maureen, that Job's comforter, again.

FOR REFLECTION

General William Booth, the founder of the Salvation Army, stated he regularly saw angels all surrounded with an aurora of rainbow light so brilliant.

Does God give his angels charge over us so that, with their help, we can get the victory over Satan?

The Apostle Paul said, 'For our struggle is not against flesh and blood, but against the rulers, against the authorities, against the powers of this dark world and against spiritual forces of evil in the heavenly realms.' (Ephes. 6:12)

'Every true believer in Christ should be encouraged and strengthened. Angels are watching; they mark your path. They superintend the events of your life and protect the interest of the Lord God, always working to promote His plans and to bring about His highest will for you.' (Billy Graham)

'We have been made a spectacle to the whole universe, to angels as well as to men.' (1 Corinthians, 4:9b)

CHAPTER TWENTY-EIGHT

Unequally Yoked

ALONG with my husband and son, then eight, I attended *Spring Harvest* in Pwllheli in North Wales. At our meal table in one of the large communal dining rooms we three were joined by five of the liveliest young folk it has ever been my pleasure to meet. There were three men in their early twenties, full of wit, and two very attractive lasses, one still in her teens. All committed Christians, the fellows, in particular, were great fun and it was sometimes difficult to get through the courses without choking with laughter. On the one occasion they overslept our breakfast was a quiet affair.

Towards the end of our time at *Spring Harvest* they gave Matthew a copy of the *Good News Bible,* each one of them having sighed it so he wouldn't forget them—as if! Matthew still uses the selfsame Bible even now in his own quiet time all these years later.

Just before we packed to return home the younger of the two girls sneaked up to our son, requesting him to find out the name of one of the Butlin's waiters.

Frankly, I wasn't too happy about her involving our son. 'Why do you want to know his name?' I asked.

'Oh, I think he's really dishy,' she giggled from behind her hand.

As she cleared one of the tables a young waitress overheard our conversation. 'Huh, you don't want to have anything to do with him,' she said. 'He's a right bad 'un.

He's only after one thing when it comes to the opposite sex. Keep well away from the likes of him—I wouldn't give him the time of day if I were you.'

My immediate reaction was to reinforce the waitress's warnings, lecturing her on the foolishness of becoming involved with a non-Christian man; but I remembered just how I detested to be lectured in my teens. I'm still not too keen on being bossed around at my age—it has always been better for me to discover things for myself, usually through the living Word of God. Try the 'Thou shalt not' approach and you won't see this rebel for dust. So it was with a softly-softly way that I approached this young beauty. I cannot remember exactly what I said, nevertheless she went away waiterless, realising she had plenty of time to find her 'Mr Right' if there was to be one. All she needed to do was to trust the one true living God who had a plan for her life. That in itself can seem easier said than done as the years spread out.

My mind flashed back to when I was her age. It was not long after I became a Christian that a non-believer invited me to go out with him. My parents strongly objected to my doing so because he was streets away from the Jewish faith.

'Why can't you find yourself a nice Jewish boy?' asked my mother, who from my birth dreamed of me having the wedding of the century and, of course, to a Jew rolling in cash.

'This young man is obviously much too old for you,' stated dad. 'Never mind his age,' interrupted mum. 'Oh, Tom, do we want our only daughter to be left on the shelf?'

Father turned to face her, explaining that the young man was at least seven years my senior and already a qualified doctor. Her countenance lit up at the thought of having a doctor in the family, but her bright happy face soon fell when I explained he was a Hindu.

I stared at them both. 'Look, I haven't even been out with him yet and you are discussing marriage, for goodness sake.'

Having had enough of their interference, I went upstairs to get ready for my date.

'We missed you at the Bible study last night, Janice,' remarked Betsy. 'Were you not well?'

'Yes. I was fine,' I replied, explaining I had been out on a date.

She raised one eyebrow and tightened her lips as had my father, displaying equal disapproval. She lectured even more than he, emphasising that, as Christians, we should not be unequally yoked with unbelievers. Out came her Bible where she read from 2 Corinthians 6:14. 'How can light and darkness live together?'

I shook my head. 'Oh, Betsy, I'm only young. I don't want to live with him. I don't want to marry him either. I just want to have a good time. Anyway, you never know, if I go out with him he might become a Christian and give up being a Hindu.'

Betsy's eyes nearly popped out of her head at the word 'Hindu' and she shook her head. It seemed everyone was trying to meddle in my young life, trying to make me old before I was young. Why did they bother over what I thought was so trivial?

On the second date (or maybe it was my third - the passing years have clouded my memory), the so-called geriatric Hindu behaved, as always, the perfect gentleman. 'It is time for me to drive you home. It was getting late and your father will be worrying if I keep you out.' As he drove his Jaguar along our gravel drive and turned off the headlights, he suggested coming in for a coffee.

'Best not,' I said.

'Why?'

'Well, you see, they are Orthodox Jews and...'

'And they will object to my colour—is that what you are trying to say?'

'Absolutely not. They would be shocked at the very idea. No, they just don't want me to go with anyone but a nice Jewish boy.'

'But, Janice, I thought you said you were a Christian,' he began, looking confused.

'I am but —' and before I could explain any further, he decided to bring the evening to a close with a goodnight kiss.

Just as he was about to touch my face an upstairs window opened and my father shouted out in the most mischievous way, 'Ethel, come on in for your mother is waiting to bath you.' And the window slammed shut.

'Ethel? Why did he call you Ethel when you told me your name is Janice? And goodness me, why does your mother still bath you at your age? Oh dear, dear me. I think it is best that we do not see each other again,' he said, shocked.

I was barely out of the car when he sped off, leaving me humiliated.

Furious, I burst into the hall and shouted angrily at my father who was doubled up with laughter. The rest of the family, now in on the joke, was shedding tears of merriment.

'That'll teach you to go out with a Hindu,' he chuckled.

Some years later, when I was a missionary in India, the full thrust of the words from 2 Corinthians 6:14-16 came home to me. I had driven the ear-shattering Land Rover belonging to the Mission to where a farmer was using two oxen of varying sizes to help plough a field. The farmer was nothing but a careless man who had been too lazy to yoke his oxen together properly. This meant that the beasts were unable to walk together in a straight line—one was pulling the other from the line and the state of the work was nothing but a wigglely mess and all because they were unequally yoked.

Charles Haddon Spurgeon is reported to have advised a young Christian girl not to marry an unbeliever.

'But surely, Mr Spurgeon, I will be able to convert him once we are married, won't I?' she asked.

Spurgeon thought for a moment and then told her to climb onto the table. 'You, my dear, represent the Christian up there and I shall represent the unbeliever down here. You try to pull me up and I will attempt to pull you down.'

He pulled her down.

MEDITATION

In the letter to the Laodicean Church we read of the Lord's loathing of lukewarmness (Rev. 3:16). But if a keen and active Christian, be he or she ever so warm in the faith, marry a cold, unwarmed Christian, then if the two are put together, even if the cold one is a little warmed, the end result is two lukewarm Christians. It is important that, if we marry, we should marry one whom we know is as eager to serve Christ as we are ourselves. Dedication to Christ should be one of the things that we look for in a potential marriage partner.

'Lord, please help me to glorify you in my use of the power to love. If it pleases you to give me a marriage partner, and children, may I excel in loving them for you. And if it is your will for me to be unmarried, may I accept this joyfully and willingly, and pour out my love for you to give fragrance to all around. In Jesus' name. Amen.'

CHAPTER TWENTY-NINE

To Russia with Love

'WHAT shall I wear for this evening?' I asked Mark on the Friday. Only I would want to know that. Other people might not care, but I was to be on show, as it were.

'Something that won't distract anyone from your talk,' he suggested.

It was a pretty vain hope and a foolish suggestion, for I didn't consider my wardrobe included clothes that did distract. I often complained to my husband that I had nothing to wear!

'But what exactly?'

Mark knew it wasn't a question of style. It was a matter of colour. 'I love you in that blue,' he said. 'Wear that.'

I wasn't being easy to please. 'I'll try it on now,' I said, and got my blue skirt and white blouse.

'You look marvellous. Now, come on.'

'You'd tell me honestly, wouldn't you?'

Mark assured me he would tell me the truth and reminded me of the time. I hate being late, in fact, I'm often much too early.

It was hard to recognise the dusty rugby hall when we arrived. The place had been transformed. Huge posters of Israel festooned the walls. There was a table covered in a white cloth which held matzos (unleavened bread) wrapped in cling film and a chalice ready for the wine. There were pink silk flowers, too, all beautifully arranged in a dry vase.

A middle-aged woman with untidy greying hair, called

Naomi, not her real name, welcomed us as we arrived. Her husband, who'd also changed his name from something gentile to something Jewish, was tuning up a guitar. Another man wearing an Oxford-blue yarmulke, but with gentile features, was clapping to the beat.

On seeing me, the guitarist came over to greet Mark and me. 'Now,' he said, 'you must be...'

'Janice... Wood,' I replied, offering my hand.

He immediately placed his right hand behind his back, declining to shake my hand. 'And you are a married woman!' he exclaimed.

Having lived so long outside Jewish circles, I had simply forgotten this particular custom. Attempting to justify myself, I reminded him that, although I had been brought up in the strict Orthodox way of life, I was now a Christian under the new covenant.

'A believer!' he quickly corrected. 'We Jews don't use the word "Christian" in this Messianic congregation.'

Knowing perfectly well that many in Messianic congregations are only partly Jewish, or Gentiles with an interest in things Jewish, I peered at his features. 'But you are not Jewish, are you?'

He flushed. 'Well, um, well, whatever, maybe I should introduce you as someone other than Janice Wood. It's so... Gentile sounding.'

'Janice is my name, and Janice Wood is my married name,' I replied. 'Wiseman was my maiden name...'

'Right! I'll introduce you... Let me think. Yes, that's it... Rebecca Wiseman! Sounds much better than Janice Wood. No one will believe you are an Orthodox Jewess with a surname like yours.'

After we'd sung some songs to which everyone clapped a lot, I, Rebecca Wiseman, gave my testimony, fully aware that two hostile rabbis were sitting immediately behind my back, hanging onto my every word.

'It was truly great to hear how Hashem (God) broke into your life,' said a chap called David.

'You come here regularly?' Mark asked him.

'Oh yes. Every Friday evening when we celebrate the start of *Shabbat.*'

'Right. So where, David, do you worship?'

'What do you mean?'

'I mean, which church do you attend?'

'Oh no. I am part of this Messianic congregation,' he said. 'I do not attend a Christian church. Neither was I baptised, as you were, Rebecca.'

'Janice,' I corrected.

'Well,' he carried on, 'we are mikvahed. Our sons, by the way, are circumcised and my lad is going to be Bar Mitzvahed. Churches just do not understand us Jews. How ever you fitted into a church I just do not know!'

'But,' I began to remonstrate, 'I thought these Messianic congregations were supposed to act as a bridge for Jews who'd come to know the Lord Jesus.'

'Yeshua... Yeshua, *not* Jesus,' he corrected me again.

'As I was saying,' I began again. 'I understood such places as these were formed to be a bridge from Judaism to Christianity. I do know folk who attend other Messianic congregations and they don't have a conflict with attending church. Here, it seems, you're going back into the Law with your prayer shawls and yarmulkes, and so on.'

Whilst I admired them for the risks they were taking in starting an evangelistic work within a Jewish area of the town, I was deeply disturbed by the emphasis they were embracing.

I knew, quite clearly, that all of the first apostles were Jewish and, whilst they frequently attended the synagogue and the temple, their important meeting together was on the first day of the week, not the seventh as in Judaism. The first day is so special because it was on the first day that the Lord Jesus rose from the dead, the one and only true Messiah. Not to lead new believers into an appreciation of worship on a Sunday, I considered was mistaken.

I wasn't invited again. But before I did leave I was provided with some information regarding the refuseniks.

'Refusenik' has become an international word to describe Soviet Jews who, having been consistently refused permission to emigrate to Israel, are harassed by the KGB (Soviet Secret Police). They are usually dismissed from their place of work and live in fear of arrest on trumped-up charges that could result in imprisonment.

After praying about the refuseniks, it was as if the Lord was telling me to get up and do something.

Three days later I contacted the Woman's Campaign for Soviet Jewry and Rita, a co-chairman, sent me a brief biography of George Belitsky, along with guidance for letter writing and literature concerning anti-Semitic propaganda in the USSR. Anti-Semitism was no novelty for even during the time of the Czars many Russian Jews were made to suffer. Stalin arrested and murdered umpteen Jewish leaders. Now anti-Semiticism was at the height of Russian fashion.

The list of refuseniks seemed endless and I knew I couldn't help them all; but I considered I could do something about George Belitsky, the longest serving Refusenik—ten years in all.

A scientist, living in Vilnius, the capital of Lithuania, George and his family first applied to emigrate to Israel in 1980 and were refused then and subsequently until early 1987 when Margaret, his wife, and Vladimir and Constantin, his two sons, were given permission to emigrate to Israel. As the sons were liable to be conscripted into the Soviet army, the family decided that Margaret and the boys would leave. George was refused permission on the grounds of 'Secrecy'. He had worked in the Institute of Mechanics until 1979, developing a measuring device that later became the subject of his doctoral thesis. When developing this device he tested it in a military installation to enter which he had to have security clearance. George was not allowed to leave the country for five years after turning in his security pass. His refusal was then extended to 2010. He was made to work as a bookbinder.

The family in Israel was adamant that George was not party to any 'Secrets' and that he should be given permission to emigrate.

At the end of 1987 Vladimir wrote, in an appeal for his father, 'It is impossible to find out which authority was responsible for the "Secrecy" in his (George's) case.'

The KGB in Lithuania claimed that the Moscow authorities were responsible for his case, and the Central authorities claimed that the authorities in Lithuania were responsible now that he lived there! George received the impression that nobody was prepared to help him emigrate to Israel.

In the meantime George became intensely conscious of the many thousands of Russian Jews who were butchered in World War II. For the seventy thousand Jews brutally killed George made seventy stars of David—one for each thousand Jews killed—and placed them before the government's official. He organised a twenty-four hour vigil and lit candles in the former ghetto area of Vilnius, so George was no meek and mild little man.

George was desperately lonely for his family and he valued support from the West. Knowing this, I either wrote letters or sent postcards every Wednesday, the day I always wrote to my once estranged Jewish family.

In March 1989 George decided to step up his campaign and held a demonstration in front of the Ministry of High

Education in Moscow. The Minister promised to review his case.

In June George had his secrecy lifted, but he was promptly sent papers for army duty for one month. This would, of course include more secrecy rating and make his emigration to Israel impossible.

On the 30th August 1989 I received two letters from George. The first said:

> Dear Janice,
>
> Thank you very much for your warm letters. I'm still a refusenik and need your help and support.
>
> Sincerely yours,
>
> Belitsky

The second letter told me he could not leave to go to Israel and begged for me to help him in his struggle. So it was I stepped up my campaign.

I began to either write to or phone every Russian Embassy that I could find on the face of the Western earth; everywhere from Canada to Luxembourg, Germany to Austria, to name but a few. I even wrote an article in one of the leading Jewish newspapers. Frankly, I didn't think it would be published, for Jews will tolerate every sort of Jew with the exception of a Messianic one. However, the editor gave me a full-page spread where I was able to make George's plight known.

Then in 1990 I discovered the Rt. Hon. William Waldegrave was leading a delegation from our Foreign Office to the Kremlin. Just before it was to leave, I placed before him information concerning George. Instead of ignoring it, Waldegrave wrote to me on 15 December 1989:

> Dear Mrs Wood,

Thank you for your letter of 22 November. I am replying as Minister responsible for relations with the Soviet Union.

We have made numerous representations about this case to the Soviet authorities in the past. We will continue to do so until there is a satisfactory outcome (the next major opportunity will be when a delegation of Foreign Office officials meet Deputy Foreign Minister Mr. Adamishin on 9/10 January next year in Moscow).

The Hon. William Waldegrave.

Less than one month after this meeting George was reunited with his family in Israel, and I have had many invitations to celebrate the Passover with him and his family.

'Next year in Jerusalem, George!'

FOR REFLECTION

Sing with joy for Jacob; shout for the foremost of the nations. Make your praises heard, and say, O Lord, save your people, the remnant of Israel.

See, I will bring them from the land of the north and gather them from the ends of the earth.

(Jeremiah 31:7-8a NIV)

CHAPTER THIRTY

Settee for Sale

I WAS sitting watching the regional news when the presenter reported that a brutal rape had taken place. A photo fit picture was shown on the screen of a man that the local police wanted to interview in connection with the crime.

'I really don't understand it,' I said, shaking my head. 'It's outrageous what's going on nowadays.'

'What?' asked my husband, obviously engrossed in a manual that would tell him how to fix our car. 'What don't you understand? What's dreadful?'

'It is dreadful that women can't go out alone at night. I remember coming in very late one night from a prayer meeting and feeling quite anxious until I was actually indoors again. Mind you, if a woman hangs about in pubs or clubs until closing time, well... she's asking for trouble, isn't she?'

He shrugged. 'Probably. I dunno. Oh, Janice, do change the subject. Such things don't affect the likes of us. By the way, what are we going to do about that old bed-settee? Should we try and get rid of it through the local rag? I know you hate it; it's so drab. Anyway, we hardly need a bed-settee when we already have enough bedrooms, do we?'

We'd inherited the drab old thing from the previous owners of the house; obviously they didn't want to take their horrible piece of furniture to their nice new home.

With my other half at work, the next day I telephoned

the local newspaper and arranged for an advertisement to be placed in the Friday issue. It was to read as follows:

Double bed-settee upholstered in sage green dralon.

No reasonable offer refused. Telephone—

No one telephoned, neither on the Friday nor on the Saturday. We were out most of the Sunday; certainly we would not have sold it on the Lord's Day.

'Well,' I shrugged, 'if no-one buys that old settee by tomorrow I'm going to phone the Council and ask them to take it away.' I did not care. I just wanted to get rid of the eyesore in our dining room.

At eleven on the Monday morning the telephone rang. 'Hello,' came a man's well-spoken voice. 'Do you still have your bed-settee for sale? You do. Oh, that's great. May I come to see it? I'd be free during my lunch break. Will you be in?'

'Yes. Yes, please do come. About 12.30 p.m.? Yes, sure, that'll be just fine.' I agreed, giving him detailed directions to our house.

Just a little before the agreed time the doorbell chimed.

'Oh, hello,' he said, offering his hand. 'I'm sorry if I'm a little early. I've come to see the bed-settee you have for sale.'

Smartly dressed, tall, well built and handsome, he was probably only in his middle to late twenties. Shaking his hand, I ushered him through the hall and into the dining room.

'What a most pleasant room,' he commented. He walked to the French windows and looked out. 'You're obviously not over looked by neighbours, are you?'

I shook my head. 'No. We're very secluded here. I'm quite pleased about that because where we used to live... well... it was a little like living in a goldfish bowl'

I directed his gaze away from the view of the garden back to the bed-settee.

'Ah, yes, that's probably going to be ideal for what I need,' he replied, running his hand over the seating.

Suddenly, he jumped and asked about a banging noise that had occurred. I smiled, assuring him that it was only the air in the central heating pipes; a plumber was expected the next day to put them right. He sounded relieved, saying that he thought there was someone else in the house. Slightly bothered by his nervous reaction, I was beginning to wish there was someone else around.

'Well, are you interested in seeing the settee, Mr... er... sorry, I didn't quite catch your name.'

He seemed absent minded, volunteering nothing about himself, but asked if I would show him how the settee opened up into a double bed. Removing the two back cushions aside, I pulled out the mattress covered springs.

He looked delighted. 'Oh, that's just ideal for my purposes. May I sit on it?'

I nodded.

As he sat on the bed, as quick as lightening he roughly snatched my right wrist and yanked me down onto him. He was very strong, much stronger than I could ever have imagined, leaving me with absolutely no hope of defending myself, preventing his violence and the subsequent rape that followed. I remember that he kept yelling at me, shouting that I should not move or he'd strangle me. Nevertheless, I tried to kick, but he hit me hard, punching me, ripping at my clothing. I managed to claw his right cheek from his eye downwards. With his face over mine, he spat at me. It was then that he pushed me aside and fled from the dining room, back through the hall, where he tidied his clothing; in no time he was out of the front door.

I climbed from the bed-settee and fell onto my hands and knees. My stomach lurched and I felt violently sick. Feeling dirty, I could not prevent the great racking sobs that tore at my body. Somehow I crawled up the stairs to the bathroom. Tearing off my remaining clothing, I showered. Still feeling dirty, I stayed in the shower for at least an hour. Drying myself, I put on my dressing gown and bundled up my soiled, ripped clothing and took it downstairs and out to the dustbin. Handling the clothing made me feel dirty again; I scrubbed my hands until they too felt sore.

'Oh, God, why, oh why have you allowed this terrible thing to happen to me? Why, God, why?' I yelled through my tears.

Trying to harness my thoughts, I sat quietly for about ten minutes, staring into space. Then it occurred to me—what if that man, that 'animal', as I called him, had passed on a sexually transmitted disease? And then... what if I became pregnant? No. Not me. The full horror of what happened, along with the possible consequences, was really hitting me hard. Maybe I needed a doctor. Yes, that's what I'd do. I'd phone our GP. William was a born-again Christian and I thought he'd be kind and understanding. Telephoning his number, he was with me within ten minutes.

He wanted to examine me, but I couldn't bear to be touched—not by him, by a man.

'Look, Janice, you really must go to the police about this matter. It's your duty. You cannot allow that man to get away with this... this terribly violent crime.'

I squinted at him and shook my head. 'They'll think I'm thoroughly bad. They'll think I egged him on, or something. After all, I did let him into the house.'

'Janice, oh Janice, you must report it. Too many rapes go unreported and then these villains get away. Let me phone the police for you. You know I'll give you all the support that I can.'

I thanked him. 'I know you will, William. You've always

been so very kind… you, your family and most of the people at the church.'

He lowered his eyes, frowned and tightened his lips.

'What's wrong?' I asked.

'Nothing, Jan; well, not exactly. I just don't think it's wise to let any of the folk from the church know about what has happened. Some may not understand. Oh, and by the way, I certainly wish to keep this matter away from my wife. I don't like her upset.'

'You don't like her upset? What about me? What do you think I'm like right now, or doesn't that matter?' I argued.

His eyes bored into mine.

'Anyway your wife is supposed to be my friend. And as for the Christians at the church… they've been like a family to me. I obviously wouldn't want to broadcast this attack to all and sundry, but if I don't have the support from God's family, then tell me, to whom do I turn?' I reasoned.

'You turn to God.'

'God and the police, eh?'

William was obviously now very annoyed by my argumentative state. He went into the hall and telephoned the local constabulary.

About twenty minutes, or so later a plain-clothes police officer, probably in his forties, arrived with a young woman police constable.

They asked me, just briefly, as to what had happened. It was so desperately painful to describe.

'What have you done with your clothing?' asked the officer. I told him and he walked out to the dustbin to collect it.

'No!', I screamed. 'I don't want my clothes brought back into the house. They're vile. They… they're … '

'I'm sorry, love, but forensic will need them. They'll also need to examine that bed-settee for… um… traces of him. By the way, you haven't showered or had a bath, have you?'

'Of course.'

The officer raised his eyes heavenwards, explaining that victims of rape should never shower. 'It doesn't help our case.'

Eventually, I accompanied them to the main police station in the town where I made a statement. After having my finger prints taken, I searched through pages and pages of mug shots. Nothing. Attempting to make up a photo fit picture of what I thought the rapist looked like, my mind went a blank. Did he have a long nose? Did he have blue or green or brown eyes? Sally, another young woman police officer gave me a cup of tea. 'I'm sorry for this must be a terrible ordeal for you. I'm afraid it's going to be a long night. Soon I'll have to take you along to our photographer.'

'Why?'

'He'll have to photograph all your bruises and grazes.'

I felt as though I'd had enough. I looked at my watch. It was 2.35 am and, bone tired, all I wanted was to curl up in bed and just sleep and sleep.

Sally put her arm around me. 'Soon I'll have to accompany you to the doctor's room. The police surgeon is on his way. He'll need to give you a thorough examination—.'

I was adamant. No man—a stranger at that—was going to lay a finger on me. 'Please, Sally, take me home—now!'

'Hey, Janice, come on now,' she said, putting her arm around me again.

'Get off! And don't "Janice" me. I tell you I' m not going to be touched, and that's that. Don't you understand plain English? Now if you don't take me home, I'll call a cab.'

Home again, I attempted to flop into bed, but somehow sleep eluded me. I lay in the bedroom, staring at the ceiling, attempting to empty my brain of every troubling thought.

'Lord,' I prayed, 'give me the sleep I so need, please.'

I slept soundly for about eight and a half-hours until my husband woke me up. 'Sorry to disturb you, but the police think they have found your attacker. They need you to go down to the station to identify him.'

I was just about to leave the house when the phone rang again. It was the duty sergeant; he informed me that the suspect in question had produced a watertight alibi. I had psyched myself up to face my attacker again, and all for nothing.

The following days, running into weeks, were awful, bringing fear and anxiety, guilt and self blame—maybe if I hadn't allowed a stranger into the house when I was alone. Sleeplessness and flashbacks took over. The slightest little noise would startle me.

I no longer attended the Sunday services, nor did I attend the usual mid-week meetings. I didn't want to leave to go out of the house, face people and be sociable. Yet I hated staying in the home when alone. William, the Christian doctor, visited me fairly regularly and he now felt I should go out and confront my fears head on. Despite all that, he still did not want either his own family or the family of God at the church to know about the rape.

'Why, William, are you so adamant regarding my keeping quiet? Surely, we are meant to bear one another's burdens, aren't we? And what if anyone comes here to the house, asking why I haven't been to the church? I'd have thought they're bound to miss me sooner or later. Anyway, it's not as though I've been immoral, or anything. Honestly, you are treating me as if I was in some way responsible. I never thought such a thing could have happened to me.'

William sighed, shaking his head. 'I think you've said quite enough, young lady,' he snapped.

The day came when I went to the 'special clinic' at the General Hospital. The clinic basically dealt with sexually transmitted diseases. I felt ashamed, angry to be there.

'We'll let you know the results of your tests in about a week,' reassured a nurse.

I hoped upon hope my tests would be negative and prayed fervently to God, pleading with him not to allow me to be anything but healthy.

I was just leaving the hospital's grounds when I saw Joanne who regularly attended the same little church as me. I tried to dart away, but it was too late; she had seen me.

'Hi, Jan, fancy seeing you here of all places. Oh dear, whatever have you been doing to yourself? You look as if you've been in the wars.'

I did not know what to say for my face was still a bit of a mess. Joanne carried on, saying that quite a lot of the people at the church had been wondering where I had been. She told me I was conspicuous by my absence.

'Look, Joanne, I hope you won't be offended, but it has been suggested that I keep quiet about what has been happening...'

Her eyes widened. 'Don't tell me your husband did that.'

'No, of course not!' I replied, almost near to tears. 'I wish I could talk to someone, but I can't.'

'Janice, we've been friends for quite a while now. I wouldn't want to intrude, but if you want a listening ear, then I'm available. Surely you can trust me. Anything you say I shall keep in confidence.'

'Thanks, Joanne, but William doesn't want me to involve any of you.'

'Blow William,' she interrupted. 'You do what you want. OK? William doesn't own you. Would you like me to come home with you?'

Once home, I explained to her that I had been unable to talk to anyone, except the police, about the rape. Even my husband and William didn't know all the gory details. When I tried to confide in Joanne she asked me to stop it because it was so horrible.

My attacker was eventually found by the CID, for he made the mistake of raping another woman in the neighbourhood soon after, and this led to his arrest.

For many years I was only too glad to let the whole thing sink into my unconscious mind. However, the mugging of a close personal friend in a London street made me realise that God's people are not immune from this kind of evil in a society where his laws are ignored. More recently I have been able to think through my rape experience again, and to wonder how many Christian women have suffered in silence, carrying a burden of guilt and shame because there was no other believer either able or willing to come alongside and counsel them through it.

It is still a mystery to me why my doctor imagined that his wife, and the little church to which I belonged, would be unable to come to terms with something like this. Was it their misunderstanding of Christian doctrine, an unwillingness to believe that anything so unsavoury could happen to someone in Christ? Why were they so helpless in the presence of happenings that were 'not nice'? Had they not read Paul's letter to the Galatians where he wrote, 'Carry each other's burdens, and in this way you will fulfil the law of Christ' (Galatians 6:2)?

Perhaps there were Christians amongst them who, had they known, would have come forward to help.

My husband and I are no longer in membership at this church and I feel that the time has come to share my experience with others of something that ought not to happen, but does.

FOR REFLECTION

For I am certain that nothing can separate us from his love: neither death nor life, neither angels nor other heavenly rulers or powers, neither the present nor the future, neither the world above nor the world below—there is nothing in all creation that will ever be able to separate us from the love of God which is ours through Christ Jesus our Lord. (Romans 8:38,39 Good News Bible)

CHAPTER THIRTY-ONE

Prisoner

ENTERTAINING a friend and colleague to a working lunch, I was ensconced in the armchair nursing a coffee when the telephone rang. 'Oh, who can that be?' I sighed.

'Auntie Janice, it's me—Tom. Something awful has happened.'

'What do you mean? Has there been some sort of an accident?'

'No. It's Danny...'

'Danny? Is he ill?'

'Oh, Auntie, Danny was arrested last night.'

'What are you talking about, Tom? Is this some sort of joke?'

'I'm telling you, Danny was arrested...'

Daniel and Thomas were special young men to us. They were so special to Mark that he'd commented on several occasions that he felt more like a dad to them, for they often stayed with us for fairly long periods of time; Tom, in particular.

When Danny was about fifteen he asked if he could earn some extra spending money. 'Have you any jobs I can do for you?'

'Well, Danny I've accidentally marked a wall in our bedroom. I was moving a chest of drawers and it left the wall with a greyish sort of line on it. A fresh lick of emulsion should sort it out, so if you want to paint that wall while we are out then you'll be a little richer than you are right now.'

Danny was not over keen to actually work that hard, but he needed cash.

'Just one thing, Danny,' I added sternly. 'You must promise me faithfully that, when you do the job, you do it alone; you bring no-one else into the house—especially members of the opposite sex. OK?'

'I promise,' he sighed, raising his eyes heavenwards.

'You really do promise, don't you?'

'I said so, didn't I?'

On returning home that evening I bumped into Chris, our next door neighbour.

'Forgive me, but I can't stop, Chris. I'm anxious to see what sort of a job Danny has made of our bedroom wall. I marked it when I moved a piece of furniture. I explained. He wanted some extra money; it shouldn't have taken him more than about three quarters of an hour, so he won't have earned a fortune.'

My husband overheard. 'Huh, knowing you, Jan, you'll give him more than he deserves. You always spoil him and Tom.'

'Three quarters of an hour!' Chris exclaimed. 'He and his girl friend have been in there for at least four hours!'

'I think you must be mistaken... you see, Dan promised me faithfully...'

Chris smirked and raised one eyebrow.

In shocked amazement, I hurried into the house and up the stairs to our bedroom. The emulsioned wall looked just perfect with a beautiful surface in vinyl silk with neither drips nor brush strokes. He certainly had performed a good job there, but then I stared at our bed. It was a crumpled mess; certainly not as I'd left it, smooth and creaseless.

By the time I'd arrived home Danny had taken the bus to his father's home, up in the Pennines about twenty miles away.

I dived across to the telephone. 'You broke your promise, Danny,' I yelled, angrily. 'You've had a girl in our bed... how dare you?'

'So what? Kelly and I were sensible...' he began.

'Sensible? What are you talking about? I trusted you. How dare you have brought her in our home when we were out... how dare you, how dare you use our bed?' I screeched down the phone.

'Ha!' he sniggered. 'I suppose you think sex is only for the confines of marriage. You Christians make me sick, and I never want anything to do with you or Mark ever again.'

In the future, all attempts to contact Danny failed and we neither saw him or Tom for three long years. We moved house a couple of times during those years and it became less likely we should see them again.

One day a friend telephoned to say she was in contact with the lads and that Danny and Tom wanted to visit us.

They were no longer awkward adolescents. Danny was a tall young man in a smart suit. Tom, at least six feet three, wore a black open necked shirt, black trousers and a coral coloured jacket. They did not look like brothers. Danny was dark eyed with tight brown curly hair. Tom was very fair with ice blue laughing eyes.

I hugged them both and, over a late meal, we chatted happily away as if the sorry past never happened. From then on our relationship with the brothers grew. There was a loving bond between us over the four years that followed.

Now Danny was behind bars. I could hardly believe it. I asked Tom what Danny had done, but he did not know all the details. He just said he thought it was something serious although no one was physically hurt. Oh not

Danny! Such a bright young man with a promising future in the field of aviation.

'He's on remand right now,' explained Tom. 'You will be able to go to the prison and see him, won't you?'

'No, Tom, I really don't think I can. If he has done some terrible thing, well, just think what the victim must feel like. I've been a victim myself and I can't tell you just how awful that feels. And then there is young Matthew to consider—I think its best that little lad knows nothing for I don't want his mind influenced in any way.'

Tom was furious with me. 'I thought you cared about him, but you don't really, do you? You don't care about either of us.'

'Of course I care about you. Oh, leave me to just get my head around all this, Tom, for it's come as quite a shock.'

Mark was as confused about this as me. Neither of us knew quite what to do, and then I hit on the idea of contacting the probation officer at the prison and asked for his advice.

'If no one but his young brother Tom visits, Daniel will feel unloved. And the unloved, the unwanted and many of those from broken or unstable homes may well reoffend. We really don't want that young man to turn to a life of crime, do we?' he said. 'With his love of money he could well do.'

The probation officer suggested that I began by writing a short note to Danny, telling him I could not condone his crime, but that I cared about him.

On prison note paper, a letter, full of remorse, came back from Danny who sounded frightened and lonely. He pleaded with me to visit him. A visit? Oh, I was unsure about that; could I handle it, especially after the attack on me? Anyway, I prayed about it, reading from Matthew 25:36-46, 'I was in prison and you came to visit me.'

I had never been in a prison before and I was anxious concerning the visit. The prison, from the outside, appeared a frightening building, imposing upon the city's landscape. The dull, scuffed waiting area for visitors was hardly a relaxing place to be with its ripped vinyl seating and dirty floors littered with empty crisp packets, sweet papers and cigarette ends. Visitors smoked under the 'no smoking' signs. Tired babies and toddlers screamed; some mothers, worn out themselves from being alone without their partners or from the long journey, shouted, swore and spanked their little ones, making the tots cry even more, creating a vicious cycle. I cringed. Suddenly, our name was being announced; we were being called in. Our outdoor clothing, my handbag and Mark's wallet went through something like the customs checks at the airports and was scanned.

'What do we do now?' I asked the warden, nervously. 'It's our first time in a prison and...'

'Just go through and sit at one of the tables and wait for the prisoner,' he replied. 'That's right, any table.'

Prisoner? Danny a prisoner? The word prisoner seemed to shoot through me like an arrow in my heart.

Mark and I walked through into the visitors' room and sat waiting. Other prisoners in blue striped shirts and denim jeans were already seated with their visitors. Some were being hugged by their friends or relatives. I was determined to hug Danny, but I hadn't a clue what I'd say to him.

Danny came through a green door and, after being searched, looked around for us.

When the twenty-minute visit came to an end, he was escorted back to his cell. I turned to wave, but he was gone.

After a couple more visits to the prison, Matthew told us he was praying for Danny in prison.

'How on earth did you know about Danny?' I asked.

Matthew began to tremble and he cried until he was

nearly sick, saying he overheard Mark and me talking. 'I wish I could go and see him in prison.'

'It's not a nice place for little boys,' I said. 'It smells. I don't think you would like it. I certainly didn't.'

'I don't care.'

'But you'd see some people in the visitors room who...'

'Mummy, I don't care. I want to see Danny.'

I contacted the probation officer once again. 'If you had a young boy would you want to take him into a prison?'

He thought for a moment or two and then said no.

However, Matthew continued to dig his heels in; he became adamant about seeing Danny.

So the day came. Matthew told Danny all about school, they chatted endlessly about computers, engines and planes. Our son, unlike us, just took it all in his stride.

The three of us visited him every month or whenever he was able to send us a visiting order. Every week we corresponded, always ending our letters with 'God bless you, Danny, and heaps of love.'

An elderly lady also wrote to him every week; when he was transferred to an open prison she wanted to send him a 'welcome to your new home' card—I stopped her just in time!

This experience with Danny has changed me. The Lord chiselled away and led me, surprisingly, into a love and understanding for offenders.

Naturally, like my rape, I hate their crime, but I have come to love them. I understand a little of when the Lord stretched out his arms and said, 'Father, forgive.'

MEDITATION

Am I a thoughtful Christian, or is my faith in a water-tight compartment, kept separate and apart?

CHAPTER THIRTY-TWO

How's your Queen?

SHORTLY after my husband, Mark, reached the official retirement age of sixty-five in 1990, we decided it would be good to 'retire' to a cottage near the North Wales coast, not too far from Llandudno where we'd spent part of our honeymoon back in the August of 1983 and had later enjoyed several short breaks.

Penrallt Baptist Church in Bangor, where the minister was then the Rev. Patrick J. Baker, soon became our 'spiritual home' for some six years. At 8.30 most Saturday mornings we joined Patrick and some of the church members for a prayer meeting. At one of those meetings, a year later in 1991, a tall, dark, visiting American, named Richard Showalter, joined us, for he was the guest preacher at both the morning and evening services during the following Lord's Day.

Next to my trip overland during the seventies which took me through eight countries, including Turkey, Iran, Iraq, Afghanistan, Pakistan, Nepal and on to India, where I became an evangelist-cum-medical missionary, I'd always wanted to visit the United States of America. Somehow, and I don't know quite why, the USA had held a fascination for me. I wasn't much interested in Disneyland and the regular tourist trails. I wanted to see small-town America; what I called the *real* America.

'So why don't you?' Richard asked, after the evening service. 'Here's my business card...'

I shrugged. 'Perhaps one day," I said, with a smile.

'Many of our Mennonite pastors would be overjoyed to have you to give your testimony to their congregations. And I'm sure all my students would be enriched.'

'Your students?'

Richard nodded and explained how he was the President of the Rosedale Bible Institute in the small town of Irwin, Ohio. (He has since moved on and is the head of the Mennonite Missions based in Pennsylvania).

My husband, who'd been half listening to the conversation, added that we, as a family, occasionally gave 'Passover demonstrations', primarily as an object lesson to demonstrate the Last Supper and how the Christian service of Holy Communion was born from it.

'Hey!' exclaimed Richard. 'That'd be really great. Think about it, you guys.'

Richard told us that Rosedale Bible Institute (RBI) was a good Mennonite Bible School, born of conviction and empowered by the Holy Spirit, equipping Christians for the ministry. 'God,' he said, 'is present in that place.'

'But, if we did visit, where would we stay…?' I began.

'No problem!'

We knew virtually nothing about the Mennonites, apart from the fact that their doctrinal beliefs were the same as the Baptists, with the exception that they were *all* pacifists… 'peaceful' folk. Mark wondered about what role he would play. How would they accept his testimony, for he had come to know the Lord Jesus Christ as his Saviour in 1945, when as a young soldier he had attended a Gospel Meeting in Cairo, convened by the Mission to Mediterranean Garrisons. Voicing these fears, Richard didn't see it as a problem. 'Just as long as you don't oppose our views on pacifism…'

'So you're serious about us visiting?'

'Yep. Sure are. Testimonies, passover demonstrations… so many of the Mennonite pastors would want you, not just in Ohio, but in New York State, Pennsylvania, Maryland, Indiana and...'

I interrupted. 'We'll think and pray about it.'

Drizzling rain hung in the air when we landed in Columbus Airport. I suppressed a whoop of joy at just being on American soil. Richard Showalter, that faithful servant of the Lord, was waiting and gave each of us a hug. As he drove us out of Columbus's busy traffic, through into the rolling rural farming land to RBI, I began to secretly wonder about Columbus.

Columbus seemed an odd choice of hero for a country that celebrates as America does, because he was such a dismal failure! Consider the facts: he made four wrong voyages to the Americas, but never once realised he wasn't in Asia. While every other explorer brought back new products like potatoes, all Columbus found to bring home were some puzzled-looking Indians—and he thought they were Japanese. But perhaps Columbus's most remarkable shortcoming was that he never actually saw the land that was to become the United States. All his voyages were spent either in the Caribbean or bouncing around the swampy coast of Central America. The Vikings actually discovered America. Yes, they did! Amazing really, for they didn't take any nonsense from anybody, which is the American way!

Just as Richard Showalter had planned, we were based in one of the R.B.I.'s staff apartments in rural Irwin, a small town in flat Ohio, well away from the usual tourist trail, where few of the locals had ever met any of us Brits in the flesh.

Having settled in the smart, two-bedroomed apartment, we desperately needed to stock up with provisions. Although there were grocery stores in the small towns of nearby Mechanicsburg and Plain City, we decided to make the twelve mile trip to Kroger's in Urbana.

Many of our out-of-town supermarkets here in Britain

cannot be regarded as small with banking services, a Post Office, a chemist and a café. However, I challenge any to compare ours with the open all hours Kroger's who seemed to have everything we have and much more, not excluding a colourful selection of artificial floral wreaths for a 'do it yourself' funeral.

If there was an Olympic medal for wandering off, my husband would have no problem in obtaining a Gold every time. 'Please, Mark, don't leave me here, not for a second, or I'll probably never find you again!' I pleaded, although I might have well been speaking to a brick wall.

I pushed a ginormous cart (shopping trolley to the likes of you and me) with the ubiquitous wobbly wheel, up and down seemingly endless aisles and, with the exception of some items such as corn flakes, I was unsure concerning some of our purchases and their prices, hoping we'd brought enough to pay for it all.

Feeling I'd just completed a half-marathon, we finally reached the check-out where the gum-chewing assistant, avoiding all eye contact, informed me in a sing-song voice of the cost. Unaccustomed to the local accent, I looked decidedly blank. She'd spoken at such a speed, I asked her to repeat herself. It was then she turned to face me full on, squinting suspiciously, as if I was stalling to pay; telling me again, I was none the wiser.

Apologising, I explained we'd only just arrived in the States and I neither understood the accent nor the money. 'See... here is what I have—please, would you just help yourself?' I asked, opening wide my dollar stuffed purse, mentally trying to convert it back to sterling.

Grinning full faced at me, the woman's mood switched to becoming overly helpful; monotonously, she counted out each dollar bill and cent, confirming she'd taken the correct amount, warning me not to invite too many folk to just help themselves!

'Awl the way from England, huh?' Hey, howdy like Ohio, then?' Oh, wow, I'd sure like t'see your wonderful country, but I'll never find the dough. I bet it's real great there, huh? Oh, and how's yer Queen, huh? Living in such a little titchy country, I betcha' git to' see her real often, huh?' she asked, bombarding me with umpteen questions, just as if we'd dropped in from outer space instead of North Wales, which she was sure was in England and a stone's throw from Switzerland!

As we began to leave, she turned and called across to a giggly check out girl seated at the next till, 'See those guys, huh? They're English.'

Confirming I wasn't deaf, I turned back and smiled at the pair.

'Have narse day,' they called to me in unison. 'Missin' yow awlready!'

Kroger's next door neighbour was Wal-Mart's—a jumbo-sized chain store, which has made its founder one of the richest men in America. It was a maze of aisles, selling jewellery, leather goods, stationery and clothing, including the brightest of orange underwear, plus just about everything you've ever combed the world's High Streets for.

It was in this shopaholic's paradise I decided to buy some tights, but the American way of sizing was, to me, a complete enigma. A middle-aged, squat and chunky woman began to stroll mindlessly by. 'Excuse me, please,' I said, stopping her in her tracks. 'Would you advise me? I need to buy...'

She glowed with pleasure. 'Well, I do declare! English, huh? Hey, I'd sure like to drop in at that Buckingham Palace of your Queen's. By the way, how's she doing these days, huh? And do y'see her real often, huh? She speaks real good English, doesn't she?'

Not again! I patiently explained how I saw her once in person at the New Year honours, and then only for about a minute or two at the most; that we commoners see her about as often as she might see the President. Trying to steer her back to the matter of my tights, and eventually succeeding, she began to roar with laughter, explaining there'd be no tights to fit me. 'Here in America tights are usually thick woolly garments for little girls to wear. I think what you want is 'panty-hose', but we usually just say "hose". Here look, these should fit you. Hey, and if you bump into your Queen, tell her Miriam-Jane Hill says "Hi". OK? Now you really won't forget, will you?'

I smiled at her naiveté, half promising to remember.

I turned to speak to Mark, but he was nowhere to be seen. In such a vast shopping scene, I didn't reckon much to my changes of finding him. I trotted up and down, searching almost every aisle, without success. I grabbed at the sleeve of a young assistant's overall; he'd just emerged from the stock room and I explained to him, in a flurry of words, that I'd lost my husband.

'Gee, I sure am real sorry about that, lady. When did he die?' he asked sympathetically. 'Was it some sort of an automobile accident? I tell yer, these here roads ain't gettin' no better.' Sombrely, he pointed me back into the direction of Kroger's flower stall where the wreaths were sold.

'No!' I exclaimed. 'He's just wandered off in this jungle and I can't find him anywhere.

'Wow, lady, where did you get that amazing accent? You ain't from around these here parts. Britain, eh? Now I…'

Before he began asking about our Queen, Mark made his appearance, only half promising not to wander off ever again. Promises are meant to be kept!

Not anxious to spend time grappling with the cooker, we dumped all our groceries in the kitchen, either in the cupboards or the fridge-freezer, and decided to make our way to the nice little town of Plain City, a short drive from Rosedale Bible Institute.

Plain City is the home of the Pennsylvania Dutch, the Amish and Mennonites. During our short time at RBI, one of the female students teased us that the Mennonites were named after a well-known brand of deodorant, but Mennonite Jewel Showalter, Richard's wife, told us that they were named after Menno Simons, one of their early leaders. In Europe they were called Anabaptists. They came to America 250 years ago. The Amish split from the Mennonites in 1693, and there have been countless subdivisions since then, but the thing that they all have in common is that they wear simple clothes; the Amish shun all modern contrivances. That's why the name of the small town was *Plain* City.

Many tourists are so fascinated by the Amish way of life, by the idea of people living 200 years in the past, that they come in their droves to gawk. Every tourist hopes to see and photograph some genuine Amish, a real offence to these people as they associate photography with the making of graven images, forbidden in the decalogue. Many of the Amish themselves have given up and moved out into the countryside, to the back roads, although they can still be seen today driving down the highways in their distinctive black buggies, with a long line of cars creeping along behind!

In Plain City we went to the Der Dutchman, one of the many barn-like, family-style Amish restaurants. The car park was packed with cars and there were people waiting inside the huge building. We debated leaving, but a tall fat man told us not to give up because it was well worth the wait. The food was that good, he said, and where food was concerned he'd clearly had some experience! Well he was right. Eventually we were ushered into the big dining room to a clean table prepared for us. Everywhere you looked the diners were shovelling food into their mouths, elbows flapping, as if they hadn't eaten for a week. Our

Mennonite waitress started to bring in the food, great platters and bowls of it—thick slabs of ham, mountains of fried chicken, 'buckets' of mashed potatoes and all kinds of vegetables. We were told to help ourselves; I heaved most of it onto my husband's plate. (He's one of those sickeningly slender types who can eat anything without putting on one ounce.) I've never seen so much food. Our young son could hardly see over the top of his plate! It was all so delicious. Just when we felt as though our stomachs were bulging, the waitress started bringing apple pies, peach pies, and bowls of home-made ice-cream.

During our meal we looked up and Elton Yutzy, one of the pastors from Maranatha Mennonite Church in Plain City, was being shown in by Janice Price, the Maitre-D. Once seated, he removed his baseball cap and, in obedience to the strong suggestion on the top of each menu, he said grace. Replacing his cap, he began to tuck in! This Amish suggestion of saying grace was observed by a group of tall, over-weight truckers who joined him at his table.

Full to bursting, we eventually stumbled zombie-like around the adjoining gift shop with its expensive array of patchwork quilts, beautifully hand-made by both the Amish and Mennonites—way outside our budget!

We got into the car, borrowed from Jewel, too full to speak, and headed towards the greenish glow of RBI where we were offered by yet another student a bucket of pop-corn!

Never say thank you in America.

We went into the bank and I made the mistake of saying thank you. 'You're welcome,' said the bank clerk. 'Have a nice day,' she said. 'Thank you,' I said. 'You're welcome.' There was no stopping it!

The Post Office, a few doors along, was no different. I asked for some stamps. 'There you are.' 'Thank you,' I replied. 'You're welcome,' she answered.

There were some lovely folk, Salina and Albert Eberly, who had the apartment below ours, and I hope when I arrive in heaven that my mansion is right next door to theirs! Salina asked if we'd spend part of Good Friday fellowshipping with them. 'Thank you, that'd be great,', I replied. 'Thank you very much. You're welcome,' she said.

The next day we called in to fill up our car with petrol at the gas station in nearby Mechanicsburg, a small-town which, compared with busy Columbus, should have been named 'Coma'. The nineteen year old man sitting behind the till was also fascinated by our British accent, promising himself to one day visit our little ol' country.

'Is your English money very different to ours?' he asked, introducing himself as William Baldwin.

I nodded and gave him some of our small change, a fifty pence piece, and so on.

He was chuffed. 'Why are you over here?'

I explained our reasons and that we were based at Rosedale. 'If you would like to call in at our apartment some time we'd be very pleased to see you, William.'

He took me at my word and one evening he turned up with a couple of submarine-sized pizzas, full of goo and spices. He also came to one of our Passover demonstrations at the nearby Mechanicsburg Mennonite Church.

The Passover is one of the miraculous events of Jewish history. It commemorates the passing of the Angel of Death over those homes which had their lintels and door posts sprinkled with the sacrificial blood, without injury to those within; whereas in those homes where this simple precaution had been neglected the first-born of the family died. It was also a perpetual reminder of the deliverance of Israel out of their bondage in Egypt. It is, therefore, a day of thanksgiving and joy.

This festival is also known as the Feast of Unleavened Bread and it lasts from the 15th to the 22nd of Nisan (See

Exodus 13:3-10) The Passover, or Seder service, as it is called, begins with the return of the head of the family from the synagogue.

We set out a table in front of the Mechanicsburg Mennonite congregation. On the table was placed an egg and three slices of unleavened bread, called matzos, hidden in a napkin. The matzos are flat biscuits, like water biscuits, but much larger. Beside those I set a bowl of salt water which was intended to represent the tears of affliction shed in the land of bondage. There was also a bunch of parsley, in lieu of hyssop, and some horseradish as a reminder of the bitterness of slavery. Finally, a mixture called *Haroseth*, which was composed of almonds, dates, apples and nuts to represent the clay from which the bricks were made in Egypt. Four cups of wine (*Ribena* in our case!) symbolised the four promises made in Exodus 6:6,7, 'I will bring you out', 'I will rid you', 'I will redeem you', and 'I will take you to me.'

The Passover story is set forth in Exodus 12. At this point, in my discourse, I stressed the spiritual significance of the feast, for in verse 13 God said, 'When I see the blood, I will pass over you.' This is important, since no lamb is slain at the Passover service nowadays. Instead there is placed on the table the burnt shank of a lamb for God did not say 'when I see your good works', or 'when I see how well you keep the Law.' No! He said, 'When I see the blood I will pass over you.'

I reminded the congregation of what Isaiah the prophet had written (Isaiah 53:6) 'All we like sheep have gone astray.' He also said 'And the Lord hath laid on him the iniquity of us all.' This method of sacrifice runs right through the *Tenach*—the Old Testament—and is continued into the New Testament where it finds its fulfilment and completion in the Lord Jesus Christ. John the Baptist summed it all up when he said 'Behold the

Lamb of God, which taketh away the sin of the world' (John 1:29)(NB All scriptures used in the Passover were taken from the AV).

'So,' spoke up one of the congregation, 'it's not only the Jews who have rejected the only way of salvation, but Gentiles, too?'

I nodded. 'It's true. Passover not only brings us all to remember a deliverance from physical bondage, but the sacrifice of Jesus Christ for the sins of the world, a deliverance from the bondage and tyranny of sin.' (Hebrews 2:15).

After the Passover demonstration, the pastor stood up and said that those who wished to be assured of their eternal salvation must accept God's way, which would be their only safeguard; it must be by accepting the sacrifice, which the Lord had provided at such infinite cost.

So I gave out an appeal. 'What will your choice be? Remember the consequences are eternal. Do not act rashly. Think first... and carefully. By accepting God's way of salvation you have everything to gain—pardon for your sin; peace with God; power to live a new life and, one day, the privilege of living in his presence for eternity.

William listened.

When it was time for us to leave the States (I didn't want the trip to be over) there was William at Columbus airport waving us good-bye.

'I'll pray for you, William. I'll write.'

'He smiled. 'Yes, please... keep in touch.'

A little while after we'd settled back in our home, we heard from Jewel, that William had started to attend the Mennonite church in Mechanicsburg, but that he hadn't made a firm commitment. We continued to pray.

The joy of joys, the following Christmas a letter dropped through our door from Irene Helmuth, another of our Rosedale friends. She told me that William had accepted the Lord Jesus Christ as his own personal Saviour; not only had he confessed with his lips, but that he'd witnessed by going through the waters of baptism. Our God is still on the throne!

In the same way, I tell you, there is rejoicing in the presence of the angels of God over one sinner who repents (Luke 15:10).

FOR REFLECTION

Joy to the world! The Lord is come!
  Let earth receive her King;
Let every heart prepare Him room,
  And heaven and nature sing.

He rules the world with truth and grace,
  And makes the nations prove
The glories of His righteousness
  The wonders of his love.

(Isaac Watts)

The King is coming again—will you be ready?

CHAPTER THIRTY-THREE

The Promises of God

WHENEVER I gave my testimony, these questions have arisen: What about your parents now? Are they still alive? After the twenty years of estrangement, have you reunited, or are they still hostile? Have they ever shown any interest in Christian things?

Almost every Wednesday I sent my estranged family newsy letters from wherever I happened to be. On special occasions such as their wedding anniversary, Passover and Hanukah, I sent cards and, on their birthdays, a present. Nevertheless, I never received any replies. At one stage it crossed my mind that they may be dead but Jane, an old school chum with whom I still kept in touch informed me that only my Granddad had passed away. Mum and dad were fine.

About six weeks before my marriage to Mark, I sent my parents a wedding invitation. Five weeks passed and we'd still heard nothing, so, through Directory Enquiries, I found out their telephone number. Hardly knowing what kind of reception I would receive, my throat felt painfully constricted as, nervously, I dialled.

'Hello,' said my dad in the refined voice he always used on the phone.

'Dad, please don't hang up. I'm phoning to ask if you're coming to our wedding. We sent you an invitation weeks ago and we hadn't heard. Please do say you'll come.'

'I dunno. Just a tick. It's best if I hand you over to your mother. Jess!' he shouted.

'Hello, dear,' she said, just as if there'd been no estrangement.

'Mum, it's about our wedding. It would make our day to have you both there.'

'Phone us again on Tuesday,' she temporised. 'Just one thing, if we do come, you know we won't take part, don't you? Dad won't give you away, but then I suppose you have someone already lined up for that.'

During the afternoon of the Tuesday before our special day yet another phone call to them confirmed they would actually be attending our wedding.

Presenting my mother with a small spray of flowers just before leaving for the church, she smiled at me. Then she turned away to fuss around the young pageboy, smoothing his fair hair, making sure that the boisterous nine year old Stephen was kept spotlessly clean. Dad, well, he just hovered awkwardly in the background, not knowing quite what he should be doing. On this occasion, the subject of our estrangement was not even mentioned, but I knew that one day it would have to surface.

One of the difficult lessons I have tried to learn in the school of discipleship has been learning how to forgive those who have wronged me. The Lord stressed the importance of forgiveness many times in his teaching ministry. He made it a condition of answered prayer in Mark's Gospel, chapter 11, verse 25: 'And when you stand praying, if you hold anything against anyone, forgive him so that your Father in heaven may forgive you your sins.'

Whilst I shall never be able to forget the traumatic experience of being rejected by my family, I have been able to forgive them and put it all behind me. It was a big help to me, being Jewish, to completely understand why they did what they did. It was the prescribed procedure— it was expected of them

Whatever had happened, it was a great joy to have them around on our wedding day.

In 1984 I told them I was pregnant and they expressed some surprise that Mark and I planned to be parents at our age; nevertheless, they were both 'over the moon' when our son was born, showering us with baby items galore from *Mothercare* and baskets of flowers.

When Matthew was almost six weeks old, we three motored the five hour journey to the south of England where they lived.

After the death of Sir John Flowers, my rabbinic grandfather, mum and dad felt free from his zealous discipline, fanatically enforced upon them throughout the whole of their married life. Granddad claimed it was ultra-Orthodoxy or nothing. So it was, after the reading of his will, they decided to auction Mulberry Court. With the sale of their own house as well, they moved to a smart apartment on the edge of Surrey, way out of the familiar Jewish area. Scrupulously maintained, it was often used to entertain dad's business associates, as well as their family and friends. (A generous man, dad had lent his name to a few worthy charities.)

As we arrived, dad was already waiting at the front door, saying nothing at first, a huge smile spreading across his face.

I smiled back. He opened the door wider, and he stepped back to one side so we could go in.

'We've missed you, Jan,' he said, tearfully, grabbing hold, wrapping his arms around me, pushing the door shut with his foot, and I knew he was really referring to the years apart. 'It has been too long. Now let's see the babe,' he went on, brushing Matthew's cheek with his lips. 'Far too long for me.'

'And me,' I said, holding on to him tightly. 'I've missed you; and mum too, you know.'

'I'm glad,' dad said, and bent his face to mine, and then releasing me, shook hands with Mark and walked us into the sitting room.

Pausing in the centre of the room, he cuddled the baby before holding him out for mum to hold. 'Gosh, it's good to see the three of you. You've put on weight,' he said to me, giving me a cheeky grin.

'That makes two of us,' I responded, laughing. 'You've turned into a butterball!'

'Ah, never mind that now. I've a bottle of champagne in the 'fridge... Dom Perignon. It's the best.' Let's have a glass.'

'Sorry, dad,' I said, sitting down on the sofa. 'But we don't...'

'Don't what?'

'Mark and I don't touch alcohol.'

'Never mind,' he said, taking away the crystal flutes. 'I've not opened it yet. Coffee be OK?'

'Thanks. Sorry about the champagne. Sorry if we've put you out.'

'I don't care,' he said, smiling broadly, his manner nonchalant. But his eyes were fastened on his new grandson.

My parents sat back on the sofa, listening attentively to any bits of news we might have had at the time, yet still focusing on the baby. I could not help but think how old they looked, dad in particular. His face, although lightly tanned, was creased and his brown wavy hair had thinned. Still stylish, his dark brown eyes were bright, full of candour and sincerity, his wide Jewish mouth was generous with smiles. For the very first time in my life I really understood how much they meant to me. Only Mark and Matthew meant more.

Lost for a few seconds in contemplation of them, I wasn't aware dad had stopped talking until Matthew let out a cry, startling me. With a jolt, I sat up straighter and blinked.

'Hey, Jan, where were you drifting off to?' dad asked, and broke into laughter. 'Were we boring you?'

'No, no, dad, you're not, honestly!' I protested, staring at him.

I wanted to tell him and mum that I loved them, but I'm not that sort of a person, not with my parents anyway.

I thought our lives would stretch out for years with them, but it was not meant to be.

At the beginning of the April, just before mum's seventy-fifth birthday, dad seemed unwell with digestive problems and he was admitted into the hospital for various tests. During his hospitalisation the skin on his heels became red and sore. First, the skin on his right heel became an open bed-sore, black and infected. The left heel soon became the same, making any mobility a pain-racked impossibility.

Throughout the next days, dad seemed to be resting more and more, sleeping for short periods of time, then he would wake to cry out in pain, pleading for stronger and stronger analgesics. He had these lapses frequently.

He rallied to sing quietly, somewhat breathlessly, 'Happy birthday' to my mother, who was with him throughout. He then lapsed into a permanent state of unconsciousness.

At 10pm on the 25th April 1996 dad died from septicaemia the source of which was his bedsores. It didn't seem fair that the parent I was getting to know all over again should have fallen prey to the stealthy invasion of this infection, leaving him exposed and unprotected, stripped of life. I don't think I'll ever stop missing him.

What I found confusing was that, back in the sixties, the Lord gave me a firm promise that he would give my parents a new heart and a new mind. He said he would take away their stubborn heart of stone and give them an obedient heart—a heart fully surrendered to him (Ezekiel 11:19). Now, as far as I knew, my father had died in his sins and gone to a lost eternity. But how could this be, for God had promised? I knew God didn't go back on his promises, and yet... Then I received a telephone call from one of the Registered Nurses who'd cared for dad during his last days. She told me that she'd had the immense joy and privilege of telling him about the Lord and, after reading to him from John 3:16, his face lit up and he accepted the Lord as his Saviour.

'I have no doubt that your father is at home in the glory, Janice, ' she said.

Truly, our God is faithful!

Dad was the owner of various successful businesses, having a finger in a number of pies, not least half a farm and a gentleman's club, but the one closest to his heart was his first grocery store, which he opened back in 1963. To him, every shopper, whether dustman or duchess, was made to feel the most special of all people. Everyone was addressed as either 'sir' or 'madam'. They were welcomed with a refreshing lack of piped music. There were clean and streamlined ranges of cook-chill cabinets. These held heat-and-eat poultry casseroles, fish dishes, and fruit and chocolate gateaux. More than 100 English and Continental cheeses were displayed on a separate counter. One of the most interesting was unpasteurised Cheddar cheese made to a 400-year-old recipe. Every day there was a tasting tray for the cheese of the day and he tried to offer cheese samples from different countries.

One of dad's customers was Sir Harry Secombe—he would call in when he was around. The two men were of the same build and their infectious laughs caused some to ask which of the two was the goon. After my father's untimely death Sir Harry wrote to my mother, and I quote:

I was so very sorry to learn of the sad passing of your dear husband Tom.

It was always my great pleasure to see him at his store in Merton Road when we would share a laugh and a chat together.

My wife Myra joins me in sending deepest sympathy and sincere condolences to you, your daughter and all those close to Tom—you will surely have wonderfully happy memories upon which to reflect once the grief has eased.

Yours,

Harry (Secombe)

Unlike the majority of Jews, dad was cremated and mum wondered what to do with his ashes. She held the jar, thinking that he didn't deserve to die, that she didn't deserve to lose him. Dad loved the noise of the sea and she wondered about taking the ashes to a sandy beach or to the open sea; but there was no hurry, she was told. She didn't have to act quickly, she could pace her time, be slow and ceremonial, without scramble and rush. Then during the early hours, a thought came to her—dad loved cricket; whether it was a County match at Lords or a local game on the village green, being there filled his summers.

With a group of those closest to him, she headed for his favourite village cricket ground. For a moment or two she stood on the pitch where the batting had often excited him. 'Good-bye, Tom, my darling,' she said, as the ash became the wind.

As for my mother, although there is an intrinsic desire to turn back the clock, still wondering how such a cruel thing could happen to her beloved, she now happily welcomes the visits of a Baptist minister into her home;

he prays with her and she is now the proud owner of a New Testament! Maybe she hasn't had a Damascus Road experience, yet I am positive that she now belongs to the Lord.

God is faithful who promised.

MEDITATION

Reveal in us your glory,
Stir in us your power,
Renew in us your kingdom,
Develop in us your faith.
Show in us your way,
Open in us your love,
Strengthen in us your hope,
Work in us your miracles,
Revive in us your resurrection.
Abide in us yourself.

(From 'Tides and Seasons' by David Adams)

Have we a deep and growing desire for a spiritual quickening in the Jewish world; indeed for all, whether Jew or gentile? Who will teach and ground them in the Word of God? Will some of the harvest be lost through lack of labourers?